A GREAT WEEKEND IN

PARIS

A GREAT WEEKEND IN PARIS

'Paris...? You're going to Paris...?' There's always a hint of envy and nostalgia in other people's voices when they ask you this question. Very few cities in the world can match its reputation for beauty and charm. On each street corner, it seems, an artist once lived or a painter was born. No other city is so firmly entrenched in the national memory, and no other city has seen so much history unfold within its boundaries. Despite attempts at decentralisation, the political decisions of France are still made here, and all the latest trends, whether passing or enduring, in fashion, philosophy and art begin in Paris.

People come from the four corners of the world to see Paris and to explore its many varied districts. It's a relatively small city, at least when compared with the sprawl of London, and its centre is very compact. This compactness, together with an excellent transport system, make Paris a very visitor-friendly city. From the imposing majesty of Notre Dame to the humblest parish church, there are many

beautiful buildings and monuments to admire.

When you explore the city, don't forget to look up as well as ahead. You'll be surprised by the wealth of ornament and detail you see there, from medieval-looking turrets to Rococo balconies and Art Nouveau window frames. Stroll around the Île Saint-Louis and watch the warm light reflected from the Seine flickering over the stone buildings. Admire the elegance and symmetry of the historic Place des Vosges, or simply relax in one of the

many cafés, drinking in the wonderful atmosphere.

You could never call this city inanimate. In fact, it's quite the opposite. Hurried and stressed Parisians rush past this lovely backdrop all day, but they still find time to enjoy the busy urban lifestyle both during the day and at night. Restaurants and brasseries, cafés and bistrot terraces are all favourite meeting places, from the first *petit noir* (strong black coffee) at the start of the day to the last glass of wine as it comes to an end.

Paris is a great centre for innovation. It produces, inspires and nurtures an immense market devoted to the ever changing worlds of arts, fashion and interior design. Architects, interior decorators and designers compete to create and fill the most original and sophisticated boutiques and galleries. Whatever is on your shopping list, whether it's a pair of shoes, a bag, a scarf or just something for the house, you'll find what you're looking for and perhaps a few things you hadn't realised you were looking for. However, if you don't want to buy anything, just enjoy the charm and diversity of the city. Whether you climb the Eiffel Tower, explore the Musée d'Orsay or the Louvre, or simply idle away your time in a pavement café, Paris is a wonderful place to spend a weekend whatever the season. You lucky thing!

How to get there

Paris is a major European city, and there are numerous ways of getting there. We've selected some of the best and most practical for you.

BY PLANE

Paris has two main airports, Orly (15km/9 miles to the south) and Roissy Charles-de-Gaulle (30km/18 miles to the north). Some international flights via Heathrow land at Orly but most land at Roissy CDG.

FLIGHTS
FROM THE UK

It is possible to get some very cheap flights from the UK to Paris – look for bargain flights in the back pages of the Sunday papers, ask at your travel agent, or try searching the web for bargain offers. The journey time from the UK is approx. 1hr. Some suggestions:

British Airways
☎ 0345 222 111
www.british-airways.com

Air France
☎ 020 8742 6600
www.airfrance.com

British Midland
☎ 0870 607 0555
www.britishmidland.com

FROM IRELAND

Sometimes the best deals are package deals, but is worth calling airlines to see if you can get a bargain. It may even be cheaper to go to London and catch a plane from there.

Aer Lingus
☎ 01 886 8888
www.aerlingus.ie
Flights from all major Irish cities.

Ryan Air
☎ 0541 569 569
www.ryanair.ie
Cheap flights from Dublin to Beauvais, Paris, which is 56km/35 miles north west of Paris. There is an express coach from the airport to the city which departs 20 mins after each arrival.

FROM THE USA
AND CANADA

There are direct flights to Paris from more than 30 cities in North America, so you are sure to find a good deal somewhere.

American Airlines
☎ 1 800 433 7300
www.americanairlines.com

Delta
☎ 1 800241 4141
www.delta-airlines.com

Air France
☎ 1 800 237 2747
www.airfrance.com

Air Canada
☎ 1 800 776 3000

FROM AUSTRALIA AND NEW ZEALAND

Despite Paris' status as a major air hub, there are no direct routes from Australia or New Zealand to Paris. It might be better to fly to London and then choose either the train or the plane to take you across the channel.
Try **Qantas** www.qantas.com
☎ 13 12 11 or
British Airways
www.british-airways.com
☎ 02 9258 3300
for direct flights to London.

CHANNEL CROSSINGS

Travel between France and England has never been easier since the Channel tunnel opened. If you want to take your car, Le Shuttle is a quick and easy option. From the UK call ☎ 0990 35 35 35 or visit their website at www.eurotunnel.com. From Calais, the drive to Paris takes about three hours.

The **Eurostar** links London's Waterloo station to the Gare de Nord in Paris in just 3 hrs, with approx. 20 trains per day. Call UK ☎ 0990 186 186; or visit the website at www.eurostar.com, to see schedules and fares. They offer discounts for those under 26, children, seniors and groups.

There are also a number of ferry companies, with frequent crossings – Dover to Calais takes about 1hr 20 mins. Call P&O (☎ 0990 980 980) or Stena (☎ 0990 70 70 70) for schedules and fares. Hovercrafts speed from Dover to Calais, and a catamaran crosses from Folkestone to Boulogne. Unless travelling by car, you could then take a train to Paris (see below).

BY TRAIN FROM WITHIN FRANCE

If you cross the Channel by ferry, the train is a good way to get to Paris quickly. It is best to reserve in advance,

particularly if you're taking a TGV. From the UK contact Rail Europe for fares and schedules at www.raileurope.com, or Eurotrain on ☎ 020 7730 3402. Ask about discounts if you are under 26, a student, have children or are a senior citizen. A 'Joker' ticket offers reductions, but it must be purchased up to 30 days in advance.(SNCF numbers in the panel on the right). Before boarding your train in France, don't forget to punch (*composter*) your ticket in one of the orange *composteur* machines, if you don't, your ticket will not be valid! All Paris' train stations have excellent bus and métro connections, so once you've arrived it will be easy to make your way on to your hotel.

BY BUS FROM THE UK

The main coach operator to Paris from the UK is **Eurolines**. The coaches leave from Victoria station and generally arrive at the Gare Routière at the Porte de la Villette in northeastern Paris. Call for information ☎ 0990 143 219 (UK) or try: www.eurolines.co.uk

BY CAR

The major motorways arrive at the *périphérique*, or ring road. Check your final destination and choose the nearest Porte (for the main road leading into Paris). Be prepared for heavy traffic. Once in the city, you will probably be better off leaving your car at the hotel or in a public parking garage, as parking can be a real nightmare.

TRAVEL IN FRANCE

(All numbers are French numbers, so if calling from abroad dial +33 and take off the first '0'.)

SNCF (National Railways)

☎ 08 36 35 35 39 (2.23F/min). Information in English. For enquiries, reservations, sales and timetable information (from 7am-9pm). Or try visiting their website at www.sncf.fr, for information on schedules and prices.

RATP (Paris' public transport company)

☎ 08 36 68 41 14 Call for 24-hour information in English regarding the métro, buses and the RER.

CURRENCY

The French franc is, of course, the currency used in France. Traveller's cheques are accepted in the larger hotels and department stores, but restaurants and shops will often ask you to change them at a bank first. Eurocheques will often be refused, however. There are no restrictions on the amount of currency you may bring into France.

FROM THE AIRPORT TO THE CITY CENTRE
From Roissy CDG: The quickest way is to take the **Roissyrail** which links to the Gare du Nord train station, St-Michel and

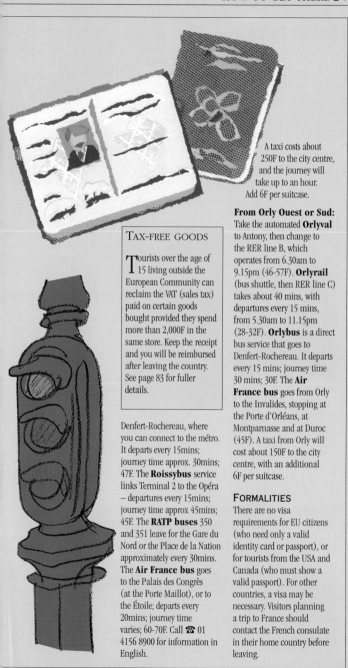

A taxi costs about 250F to the city centre, and the journey will take up to an hour. Add 6F per suitcase.

From Orly Ouest or Sud:
Take the automated **Orlyval** to Antony, then change to the RER line B, which operates from 6.30am to 9.15pm (46-57F). **Orlyrail** (bus shuttle, then RER line C) takes about 40 mins, with departures every 15 mins, from 5.30am to 11.15pm (28-32F). **Orlybus** is a direct bus service that goes to Denfert-Rochereau. It departs every 15 mins; journey time 30 mins; 30F. The **Air France bus** goes from Orly to the Invalides, stopping at the Porte d'Orléans, at Montparnasse and at Duroc (45F). A taxi from Orly will cost about 150F to the city centre, with an additional 6F per suitcase.

FORMALITIES

There are no visa requirements for EU citizens (who need only a valid identity card or passport), or for tourists from the USA and Canada (who must show a valid passport). For other countries, a visa may be necessary. Visitors planning a trip to France should contact the French consulate in their home country before leaving.

TAX-FREE GOODS

Tourists over the age of 15 living outside the European Community can reclaim the VAT (sales tax) paid on certain goods bought provided they spend more than 2,000F in the same store. Keep the receipt and you will be reimbursed after leaving the country. See page 83 for fuller details.

Denfert-Rochereau, where you can connect to the métro. It departs every 15mins; journey time approx. 30mins; 47F. The **Roissybus** service links Terminal 2 to the Opéra – departures every 15mins; journey time approx 45mins; 45F. The **RATP buses** 350 and 351 leave for the Gare du Nord or the Place de la Nation approximately every 30mins. The **Air France bus** goes to the Palais des Congrès (at the Porte Maillot), or to the Étoile; departs every 20mins; journey time varies; 60-70F. Call ☎ 01 4156 8900 for information in English.

SCENIC PARIS

'All the world's a stage,' and Paris is no exception. It's an international showcase for the arts. Feast your eyes on its palaces, monuments and churches, reflecting a time when artistic patronage and religious conviction created some true works of art. The museums house magnificent collections, and you can enjoy looking at paintings, antiques, fashion and design all over the city, whilst shop windows are often works of art in their own right.

AROUND THE SEINE

The Seine is both the heart and mirror of Paris. A river trip will take you back in time. Visiting Notre Dame and the surrounding streets is like stepping into the Middle Ages. Île Saint-Louis and the Marais area are steeped in 17th-century history. The Louvre was once the setting for royal splendour,

and the Conciergerie witnessed the last days of the royal family during the revolution. Place de la Concorde is a prime example of sophisticated 18th-century architecture, and the Grand Palais and the Petit Palais are lavish in style, especially when compared with the more sober Invalides. The imposing Palais de Chaillot was built for the last Universal Exhibition.

THE INTERNATIONAL SCENE

Paris is a trendsetting city, a maker and breaker of fashions, yet at the same time it's open to new influences from around the world. It's probably the only city in France where you can step through a doorway and find yourself in a foreign land. The Russian community has its own churches, food shops and restaurants here, and the Rue du Faubourg Saint-Denis is home to many Pakistanis and Sri Lankans. The famous Rue des Rosiers is the traditional heart of the Jewish quarter, whereas the shops in Barbès and La Chapelle have the atmosphere of a souk. You'll think you have been transported to Asia if you visit the Avenue de Choisy or Belleville, where the many Vietnamese shops display their exotic fruits on the pavement.

SETTING THE STAGE

The most fashionable Parisian designers are responsible for the interiors of many galleries, boutiques, cafés and restaurants. Marketing and sophistication have joined forces to create *the* places to go to be seen. Andrée Putman designed the Et Vous stores.

in the Rue Royale; the Esprit shop is the work of Italian designer, Citterio; Willmotte was the creator of Junko Koshino; Garouste and Bonetti designed rooms for the couturier Christian Lacroix; Jean-Paul Gaultier created the Gaultier gallery in the Faubourg Saint-Antoine; Olivier Gagnère designed the Bernardaud tearoom, and Elizabeth de Portzamparc the café at the Cité de la Musique.

BEHIND THE SCENES

Paris is full of hidden treasures. Push open a door and you

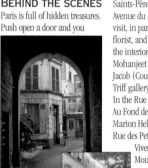

may discover a delightful courtyard, where 100-year-old trees shade lovely old buildings. Shops and studios now often occupy these old courtyards. Visit the Étoile d'or, the 18th-century workers' houses, Rue du Faubourg Saint-Antoine (no. 75) or the Arbre à Lettres bookstore (no. 62).

See the glass-roofed Casal fabric store at no. 40 Rue des Saints-Pères. The studios at 21, Avenue du Maine are worth a visit, in particular Lieu-Dit, the florist, and William Foucault, the interior decorator. Visit the Mohanjeet gallery in the Rue Jacob (Cour de Saxe) and the Triff gallery (no. 12 and 35). In the Rue de Seine, don't miss Au Fond de la Cour at no. 49. Marion Held Javal at no. 5, Rue des Petits-Champs, and Vivement Jeudi, 52, Rue Mouffetard, are other good places to visit.

THE ITALIAN INFLUENCE

There's a little bit of Italy on every street corner. Armani has a store on the Place Vendôme near the Ritz and another on Place Saint-Germain-des-Prés. Prada, Sergio Rossi, Fausto Santini, Angelo Tarlazzi and Max Mara all show their collections from the Rue de Grenelle to the Rue du Cherche-Midi. Gianfranco Ferre is on Avenue Georges-V, and Versace is on the Faubourg Saint-Honoré, near Hermès. There are also plenty of Italian grocers, caterers and restaurants.

DEYROLLE BOUTIQUE

Deyrolle is an unusual and timeless place. For the last two centuries, it has been a favourite haunt for nature lovers, who come to see its treasure trove of insects, gems, minerals and stuffed animals, which is unique in Europe. There are lions, crocodiles and snakes, all frozen in time, fabulously coloured butterflies from Ecuador and ornate intricate shells from the Pacific. Deyrolle is at 46, Rue du Bac, near the Rue-du-Bac metro station.

PARIS ARCADES

Arcades are a Parisian invention and are known as *galeries* or *passages*. They thread their way between houses or form secret passageways from one street to another. They became fashionable during the Restoration, aided by property speculation, and became popular rendezvous, places to see and be seen. Nowadays, even if the crowds have gone, they are still full of the kind of charm and mystery which appeals to the Parisian soul.

IN THE BEGINNING

In 1785, the Duke of Orléans was in need of money and decided to sell the arcades he had constructed in his garden at the Palais-Royal. He linked the Galerie de Montpensier to the Galerie de Valois with a wooden bridge, on which a variety of merchants soon set up shop. The arcade was born, and it became an instant success. Indeed, after the Revolution, speculators copied the idea, buying up the land that had become available through the sale of state property to build more arcades.

THE GOOD TIMES

The Vivienne, Colbert and Véro-Dodat Galleries opened in 1826. Glass roofs replaced the skylights which had originally studded the ceilings, wooden posts were removed to make the windows larger, and the use of cast-iron made the structures more solid. From 1817, the arcades were lit by gas light. People flocked to the restaurants and cafés, the book shops and reading-rooms, the cake shops and sweet shops. Milliners and dressmakers also set up shop. The bourgeoisie, dazzled by such newly accessible luxury, spent lavishly and enjoyed the elegant evening balls held there.

THE DECLINE. . .

When Louis-Philippe was on the throne, he put an end to

the prostitution and gambling which were rife in the gardens of the Palais-Royal. This signalled the end for the other arcades too. Under Napoleon III, the capital was increasingly urbanised and modernised. Spectacular new buildings were constructed, and Parisians gradually turned away from the previous focus of their interest. What had once inspired their enthusiasm had now become outmoded. In the 1878 Baedeker guide, the Parisian arcades were not even given a mention. Arcades sadly, became history.

BACK IN FASHION

The arcades have now been renovated and are attracting

. . . AND FALL

The years passed. By the early 1960s, the Galerie Colbert was being used as a warehouse, and its rotunda was little more than a car park. When the glass roof of the Galerie Vivienne collapsed under the weight of the workman who was repairing it, nobody seemed to be interested. However, during the 1980s, fashion houses moved into the Place des Victoires and fabric designers into the Rue du Mail and the Rue des Petits-Champs. Parisians began to rediscover the charm of the covered arcades in this district, almost totally forgotten since the previous century.

crowds once more. The little shops Balzac described in *Les Illusions Perdues* have been replaced by interior design and fashion boutiques, which have moved in next to the remaining booksellers, secondhand dealers and craftshops. The old cafés are busy again, and new ones have

opened. The world of designers, couturiers, journalists, advertising executives and their entourages now use the arcades as meeting-places, reviving an old tradition which appeared, until recently, to have died out.

WHICH ARCADE TO CHOOSE?

For fashion, home decoration and books try Galerie Vivienne (see p. 41). Passage Choiseul has an interesting mix of clothes and toy shops, poster shops, phone boutiques and the like. Visit the stylish Galerie Véro-Dodat (see p. 40) for secondhand or antique dealers and leather goods. The Panoramas arcade (between the Rue Saint-Marc and Boulevard Montmartre) is worth a visit and is a good place for lunch or a quick coffee break. In Passage Jouffroy, there are lots of interesting things to see, in particular, Thomas Boog and Pain d'Epices which are both full of great ideas. You will also enjoy a stroll in the Verdeau arcade, especially if you are keen on drawings, engravings, old books and postcards.

PARIS IN BLOOM

April in Paris is not the only time to enjoy its wonderful flowers and no-one prepares a bouquet quite like a French florist, as you'll see if you buy flowers to give as a gift. You could even do a 'floral tour' of the city, which would wind its way from florist to florist, taking you through markets and public gardens and along the tree-lined avenues. It would be a novel way to visit the capital, whose colours and scents change with the seasons.

TOWN AND COUNTRY

As early as the 17th century, the elegant buildings in the Marais had beautiful gardens. Marie de Médicis' Luxembourg Gardens, which were a favourite of 18th-century writers and artists, have hardly changed since Chalgrin completed them in the early 1800s. The present layout of the Tuileries is now similar to Le Nôtre's original design,

and when Paris celebrated the bicentennial of the Revolution, the Champs-

Élysées was transformed into an enormous field of wheat, successfully transporting a symbol of France's agricultural riches into the heart of its capital.

THE PERFECT SITE

Paris is well qualified to be a 'flower capital'. It's a city with wealth, a long tradition of good taste and a deep nostalgia for the countryside. It is also situated right at the heart of a horticultural region. Even its sprawling suburban development has not destroyed this tradition. The names of southern suburbs, such as Belle Épine, l'Hay-les-Roses and Fontenay-aux-Roses, remind us that this is still the rose-growing centre of the country. The Vexin area is the source of the bulbs which colour the capital all year

round, and masses of flowers arrive daily from southern France to the Paris airports, just 30 minutes outside the city.

PUBLIC GARDENS

The City Council gardeners lovingly look after the flower beds and borders in the 400 or so public gardens and avenues. The flowers lining the paths in the Luxembourg

Gardens change with the seasons and the Champs-Élysées has stunning floral displays all year round. The Bagatelle park is famous for its roses and 100-year-old trees, and the Jardin des Plantes boasts a huge variety of species. The floral park at Vincennes is a must when it is ablaze with stocks, tulips, pansies and a unique collection of irises. Nearly 100,000 plants are grown every year in the magnificent Auteuil greenhouses, which were constructed during Napoleon III's reign.

GREEN STATISTICS

The City Council looks after some 7,600 acres of parks and gardens, and an impressive 600,000 trees, which equals one tree per 3.5 Parisians. Every year, the municipal gardeners plant 3,100 new trees, 215,000 perennials and climbing plants, and 3,000,000 green or flowering plants. Whenever they can save a green space or add a touch of nature to the urban

environment, landscape gardeners do all they can, with varying degrees of success. Such areas can be found at Les Halles, the André Citroën park, the Belleville garden, the Parc de La Villette and the Bassin de l'Arsenal waterside development. The most recent acquisition is the 'green trail' (*coulée verte*) along the Daumesnil viaduct, which runs from the Bastille to the forest of Vincennes.

THE POWER OF FLOWERS

Flowers and gardens play an important part in today's modern lifestyle, with people striving to reduce the stress in their lives and live in a more natural and harmonious environment. You can buy bouquets of flowers at specialist markets, but we have made a selection of the best Parisian florists for you to try:

∎ **Christian Tortu**
6, Carrefour de l'Odéon, 75006 ☎ 01 43 26 02 56
∎ **Marianne Robic**
41, Rue de Bourgogne, 75007 ☎ 01 44 18 03 47
∎ **Michel Léger**
69, Rue de Grenelle, 75007 ☎ 01 45 49 09 70
∎ **Liliane François**
64, Rue de Longchamp, 75016 ☎ 01 47 27 51 52
∎ **Olivier Pitou**
23, Rue des Saints-Pères, 75006 ☎ 01 42 27 97 49

∎ **Lambert-Bayard**
6, Rue du Renard, 75004 ☎ 01 42 72 17 40

MONCEAU FLEURS

84, Blvd Raspail, 75006
☎ 01 45 48 70 10
Metro Saint Placide or Rennes
Open Mon.-Sat. 9am-8pm,
Sun. 9.30am-1.30pm.
And also:
11, Blvd Henri IV 75004,
92, Blvd Malesherbes 75008
60, Ave. Paul Doumer 75016
2, Pl. du Gal Koening, 75017
94, Blvd des Invalides 75007

This is the chain of florists that Parisians prefer. The choice is huge, the flowers always fresh and the prices unbeatable. You can often find beautiful roses from 5F each, and for just 100F you can buy a magnificent bouquet.

INTELLECTUAL PARIS

'France is the oven in which the bread of man's intellect is baked," or so said the Cardinal Eudes de Châteauroux in the 13th century. Paris became the country's capital in 987 with the coronation of Hugues Capet, and its reputation as a city of ideas, philosophical trends, literary and artistic creativity, and of protest movements, has always reached far beyond its own frontiers. France's publishers, bookshops, press groups and media companies choose to be in Paris. The intelligentsia still gather at dinner parties, and cafés and restaurants remember the golden age when they were frequented by the likes of Sartre, Cocteau or Fitzgerald.

THE PROLOGUE

In the Middle Ages, the finest minds were attracted to the capital. People came from the provinces or abroad to study in Paris, and many colleges grew up around the Sorbonne, which opened in 1257. The Latin Quarter (so-called because teachers taught in Latin) became the centre of all intellectual activity. Its reputation grew with the founding of the Collège de France in 1530. These universities then attracted the publishing industry to this quarter.

BRANCHING OUT

The intellectual influence of Paris continued to spread. The French kings acquired an entourage of intellectuals, scientists and artists. French philosophers exported their ideas during the 18th century. Voltaire and Rousseau were known throughout Europe, foreign courts modelled themselves on Versailles, and Parisian salons were famous

for their wit and humour. The 19th century saw the genius of writers like Balzac, Zola, Flaubert and Eugène Sue, whilst the early 20th century was captured forever in the pages of Proust.

BOOKSELLERS

The Parisian booksellers or *bouquinistes* played an important role in the circulation of books. In 1857, there were 68, and one, a

certain M. Laîné, is known to have handled nearly 150,000 volumes every year. Bookshops such as we know them today did not yet exist, but there were 'reading rooms' and 'literary salons", which were often part of publishing houses. Books could be borrowed there for a fee, and intellectuals met to read the latest publications, or to settle into a comfortable armchair and devour the foreign press – much like Stendhal, who used to frequent the Galignani bookshops.

SOMETHING FOR EVERYONE

One of the advantages of being in Paris is that you can find any book you're looking for. Theatre fans spend hours at the Librairie Théatrale (3, Rue Marivaux, 75002 ☎ 01 42 96 89 42) or at

WRITERS AND ARTISTS

The streets of the Left Bank are full of memories. Balzac took up printing and publishing at 17, Rue Visconti, before starting to write. Racine spent the last years of his life at no. 24 of the same street. Delacroix painted at the Place de Furstenberg. L'Hôtel in the Rue des Beaux-Arts will always be linked to Oscar Wilde. Abbot Prévost, author of *Manon Lescaut*, lived at 12, Rue Saint-Séverin; Alphonse Daudet and Charles Cros at 7, Rue de Tournon. Pascal wrote his Pensées at 54, Rue Monsieur- le-Prince; Sainte-Beuve lived in the Cour du Commerce Saint-André, and Verlaine in the Rue de la Harpe.

the Entrée des Artistes (161, Rue Saint-Martin, 75003 ☎ 01 48 87 78 58), where they are greeted on arrival by an extraordinary collection of automata. Globetrotters (real or armchair) can dream at the Astrolabe (14, Rue Serpente, 75006 ☎ 01 46 33 80 06), or at Ulysse (26, Rue Saint-Louis-en-l'Ile, 75004 ☎ 01 43 25 17 35). The Librairie Gourmande (4, Rue Dante, 75005 ☎ 01 43 54 37 27) is a great place for gourmets to devour books. And gardeners find it hard to resist the Maison Rustique (26, Rue Jacob, 75006, ☎ 01 43 34 96 60).

THE LEFT BANK

When Abélard (1079-1142), considered to be the first French philosopher, was ousted by the canons of Notre-Dame, he crossed the Seine with his students and began to teach on the Left Bank. The Latin Quarter was born. Nowadays, despite the proliferation of universities and faculties in the outskirts of Paris, the fifth and sixth *arrondissements* are still an important centre for students, with plenty of busy cafés, alternative cinemas, and university bookshops. Any self-respecting member of the Parisian intelligentsia lives around there too.

CAFÉ SOCIETY

Paris would not be Paris without its cafés. From Trocadéro to Saint-Germain, from Montparnasse to the Bastille, they have been the silent witnesses to the city's most interesting, and sometimes most creative and inspirational, conversations and debates. In the 18th century, Voltaire and Rousseau met at the Procope café in the Rue des Fosses-Saint-Germain. The tradition continues today, and great ideas are still conceived over a glass of French wine in a smokey café.

CAFÉS AND POLITICS

The cafe soon became an ideal place for debating fashionable ideas. Diderot and d'Alembert are said to have launched their great philosophical work, the

Encyclopédie, at the Procope and revolutionaries frequented the cafés of the Palais-Royal, led by Camille Desmoulins. In the 19th century, the Tortoni café was a popular meeting place for great minds, and later Trotsky chose the Closerie des Lilas as his favourite place for preaching his philosophy. The Café de Flore became famous through its customers, Jean-Paul Sartre

THE FIRST CAFÉ

Venice and Marseille were enjoying café life quite some time before Paris, which had to wait until 1684 for its first café. It was opened by a Sicilian, Francesco Procopio, and was an instant and huge success. The theatre company, the *Comédie Française*, set up on the opposite side of the street, and theatre-goers began to stop at the Procope café between shows to enjoy the newly imported drink from the East. Racine is reputed to have written his plays, cup of coffee in hand.

the pavements, leaving just enough room for pedestrians (entitled to a width of 1.4-1.6 metres, as decreed by the City Council). The Americans who discovered Paris after World War II were delighted by these impromptu terraces. They are featured in many films from the 1950s, including *An American in Paris* and *Funny Face.* Parisian terraces, whether those of fashionable cafés or traditional bistrots, have a charm all of their own. They are places to see and to be seen. The ultimate in chic at the moment is to carry on an important telephone conversation on your mobile phone, while your lunch companions wait for you to finish, pretending not to listen.

A SHORT HISTORY OF THE BISTROT

Towards the end of the Russian retreat in March of 1814, the Cossacks pursued Napoleon's armies into Paris, which was then occupied by Russians, Prussians and Austrians. The French word *bistrot* originates fom this period. When they wanted to have a quick drink, the Cossacks went into inns and taverns shouting 'bistrot, bistrot...', which means 'quick' in Russian. Today, Paris bistrots tend to be small, moderately-priced restaurants with a limited, but often very good, selection of food.

and Ernest Hemingway had regular tables at the Closerie des Lilas and also went to the Café de Flore, as did André Breton, Albert Camus and others. Their conversations and observations in such surroundings often gave birth to a new novel or play.

PARISIAN TERRACES

When the sun shines, the tables come out of the cafés onto

WAITER!

In certain establishments through the late 1930s, it was customary for Parisian café waiters to buy their own aprons. The traditional outfit is a black bow-tie, a white waistcoat, a long white apron reaching down to the shoes, or a white jacket and black trousers. A waiter can walk long distances each day on his rounds from one table to another. They are often the customer's confidante, privy to all kinds of secrets, but totally discreet. Each year on a Sunday in mid-June, the City Council and the Syndicate of Café Owners organise a 'waiters' and waitresses' race', when the public can admire their speed and skill, as they carry a trayful of drinks through the streets of the capital.

and Simone de Beauvoir, who developed their existentialist philosophy at the café over a glass of wine.

ARTISTS' CAFÉS

The cafés in Montparnasse and Saint-Germain-des-Prés were regular watering holes for writers and painters. Apollinaire went from one café to another and Modigliani paid his debts at La Rotonde with a total of 14 paintings, which were burnt when he died. Truman Capote

GOURMET PARIS

France is a country of natural riches in which agriculture, farming and fishing are of great national importance. It's no surprise then that Paris is a gourmet's paradise. In the past, kings employed the best chefs, and master pastry-makers invented the delicious cakes we still enjoy today. There are many references in literature to markets overflowing with produce and fashionable, culinary extravaganzas. Patisserie windows will be a source of constant temptation. Give in and enjoy the flavours of Paris.

foreign flavours. Hédiard started the trend in 1860, with the 'Spices and Colonies Counter' in the Rue Notre-Dame-de-Lorette, which sold unfamiliar spices and exotic fruits and vegetables. In 1886, Auguste Fauchon set up his

fruit and vegetable stall at the Place de la Madeleine, and Parisians flocked to taste his new and unusual produce. The rest is history.

Les Halles in the 19th century.

THE 'BELLY' OF PARIS

In 1855, at the request of Napoleon III, the architect Baltard designed the huge iron construction known as 'Les Halles''. This central food market became an important feature of the city. The late-night customers in the nearby restaurants and bars would mingle in the early hours with the market-workers. In 1969, when Les Halles moved out to Rungis on the outskirts of the city, something of the soul of Paris went with them. Today, the market covers 232 hectares, and some 28,000 vehicles leave daily with food supplies to feed one-fifth of the population of France.

DELICATESSENS

A new kind of grocery opened its doors in the 19th century, and Parisians began to enjoy

A SWEET TRADITION

In the 16th century, the pastry maker would sing about his wares in the streets, drawing in customers. In 17th century

Paris, Ragueneau invented the *amandine*, a delicious almond tart, and Vatel concocted Chantilly cream. In the 1800s, Carême first made nougat and meringues. The fondant made its appearance in 1830, followed by candied chestnuts in 1835. During the same period, the Sergent cake-shop in the Rue du Bac was famous for its *millefeuille*, and a certain M. Quillet made the first butter cream in 1865.

CHOCOLATE LOVERS

Anne of Austria first brought chocolate to Paris via Spain

and the conquistadors. The first manufacturer of chocolate liqueurs and pastilles opened its doors in 1659. It was the ultimate in chic, and the Marquise de Sévigné mentioned it in her letters. Nowadays, Paris boasts many exceptional chocolate-makers: Robert Linxe, Christian Constant, Pierre Hermé for Fauchon, Dalloyau, Lenôtre, Debauve and Gallais. On winter afternoons, locals and tourists queue together to taste the rich and creamy hot-chocolate drink served in the famous *Angélina* tearoom. Paris even has a Chocolate-Crunchers' Club for chocaholics.

A TASTE FOR THE EXOTIC

Paris is the only city in France where it's just so easy to find food from all over the world, including Africa and the West Indies, Asia and the Mediterranean, America and Russia, the Near East and Scandinavia. There are more and more specialist food stores, catering to the widest variety of tastes and introducing the cream of foreign gourmet traditions to

the Parisians. Fruits, vegetables, spices, condiments, charcuterie and pastries – you have the whole world on your plate.

LET THEM EAT CAKE

Even though it's served in cafés at breakfast time with coffee all over Paris, the famous *croissant* is far from Parisian in origin. It is, in fact, one of the appropriately named 'Viennoiseries", imported from Austria. As for the *brioche*, it was invented in 1690 in Paris, as was the *baguette* which first appeared in the 1960s. The larger *pain*, is also Parisian in origin, and it is made from white flour kneaded in particularly expert way.

TREASURE HUNTER'S PARIS

Saturday mornings are for treasure hunters in Paris. After a *petit noir,* head off to the flea markets. You'll find a vast array of furniture and objects piled on shelves, spilling onto the pavements and into the road. Start hunting and who knows what you might uncover.

FLEA MARKET STYLE

Appearances can be deceptive—don't be fooled by the stallholder who's playing cards, or sharing a picnic with his mates at a stall that seems to be full of junk. He may be a well-heeled aristocrat in disguise, who loves the flea market and its unique atmosphere, together with the lure of a good find. Don't expect to find the most fantastic bargains. You're dealing with a professional who knows his stuff and is aware of what it's worth. Dress casually and cultivate a relaxed and almost indifferent air, and never let on what you're looking for.

and dance hall crowds, and on their way they stopped to look at the extraordinary piles of rags and bric-a-brac. They soon took more than just a passing interest and began to buy. A new fashion was started, and in 1891 the flea market was born. It has continued to grow ever since.

THE HISTORY OF THE FLEA MARKET

It all started with the rag merchants who set up in the late 19th century outside the city walls, in order to avoid paying the toll that was levied inside the city. They chose Saint-Ouen because the Montmartre locals passed through there on their way down to the dance halls. A certain section of bourgeoisie, always on the lookout for excitement, came here to rough it with the café

TIPS ON SAINT-OUEN FLEA MARKET: WHAT'S WHAT

Everyone goes to Saint-Ouen. People from all walks of life can be seen at the countless stalls of the ten markets (not counting the *Usine*, which is for professionals only), covering nearly 76 acres. It's the world's largest antiques market. It's not worth getting up at the crack of dawn to come here, as most stalls open at about 9 or 9.30am on Saturdays, Sundays and Mondays, and close at 6pm. The markets all have a different flavour. Vernaison has something for everyone, from jewellery to lighting, while Biron is more expensive, with furniture for wholesalers from New York's East Side. At the Serpette market, certain stallholders tend to specialise in 1930s pieces. Paul Bert is still the most authentic flea market, where you can look around and hunt through things yourself, and many designers and decorators come here. For leather jackets, jeans, Doc Martens, (and, beware, the odd pickpocket), go to the Malik market. And when you're ready to drop and longing for lunch, take a break in one of the many cafés or restaurants, avoiding the lunch-time rush hour if you possibly can. (For information on other flea markets, see p. 112.)

WHAT TO BUY, HOW TO PAY

There's no point in offering 10,000F for a table if the asking price is 20,000F. It's better to compare prices, and consider how much an object is worth before you start haggling. You often get better results by chatting with the stallholder and establishing a friendly rapport. It also helps if you pay cash. Don't hesitate to go away and come back ten minutes later. It's unlikely the object of your desire will disappear. They will hold it for you, or let you pay in instalments. If it's expensive, you should ask for a dated and detailed invoice, which makes things easier for the insurance forms if you resell it, or if it is stolen.

the parapets and padlocked to protect their contents, old books, papers, engravings, postcards and posters. The collections are of mixed interest and quality, but if you take the time to look, ignoring the noise and pollution from the passing cars, you just may chance upon that special something.

THE BOUQUINISTES

From Quai de la Tournelle to Quai Voltaire on the Left Bank, and from Quai de l'Hôtel-de-Ville to Quai du Louvre on the Right Bank, the secondhand booksellers, or *bouquinistes,* are all part of the special charm of Paris. They've been there as long as the Pont-Neuf, constructed by Henri IV. Their lacquered green wooden boxes are secured to

PARIS FASHION

Only in Paris do some 2,000 journalists and 800 buyers gather together when the haute-couture and ready-to-wear collections go on show. Karl Lagerfeld may be German, John Galliano, British, and Gianfranco Ferre, Italian, but Paris is still the fashion capital of the world. Asians and Americans come twice a year, to be among the first to see the new designs which will be worn from the Pacific to the Atlantic. Parisian chic is still in a class of its own.

Christian Lacroix Haute Couture hiver 97

FASHION SHOWS

The ritual fashion shows, at which couturiers from all over the world present the results of months of work, are now held at the Carrousel du Louvre. It's the same every year—people crowd at the door, rush to their seats, look around to see who's there, and then wait in excited anticipation. The atmosphere is electric, while behind the scenes the tension grows. Then on come the spotlights, the music starts, and the world's top models step out onto the catwalk. The shows are wonderful publicity for other industries such as accessories, perfumes and cosmetics.

THE BUYERS

After the last war, there were around 20,000 women wearing haute couture clothes. Now they can be counted in their hundreds only. Almost 80% of the clientèle is foreign, primarily American, then Asian and European. Middle Eastern women used to be big customers, but less so since the Gulf War. A couturier dress requires at least 100 hours of extremely painstaking work and three or four fittings. It will cost more than 50,000F, while an evening dress can be four times as much. This is why haute-couture only accounts for 6% of couturiers' real turnover. However, these prestigious creations are still fantastic publicity for the fashion houses' less exclusive productions.

DESIGN AND MARKETING

To keep up with social and economic changes in society,

fashion designers and couturiers now develop a wide range of accessories and ready-to-wear clothes. This trend began back in the 1970s, a period when 15-25 year olds really began to count in the marketplace, both as consumers (even if their buying power was relatively limited) and fashion-makers in their own right. New names came to the fore, and designers took note of the needs of this new clientèle. Kenzo, Agnès B.,

Dorothée Bis, Emanuelle Khanh, as well as Yamamoto and Comme des Garçons set up in Paris. Young people began to adopt an informal style which soon became the uniform in

In 1997, 68,000 faked articles were seized, but Italy continues to break production records and Indonesia, Thailand and the Philippines still flood the market with fakes. As a result, French companies spend a lot of money trying to protect their products.

universities and trendy cafés, consisting principally of casual shirts and jeans.

FAKES

There is always a price to pay for fame, and for haute-couture, it means copies of your product being made abroad. Some people will go to any lengths to wear a famous name. Imitations can be found at a fraction of the price, but the mediocre quality ultimately harms the reputation and image of the original, and is damaging both for the economy and for the export trade. The customs authorities and the police keep a sharp lookout.

LUXURIOUS PARIS

In the 19th century, the perfumes from the house of Guerlain were worn by many beautiful women whilst it was Poiret who dressed the fashionable Parisians in the Roaring Twenties. Just a mention of the names Dior, Hermès, Cartier and Lalique conjures up images of French luxury and chic, much envied outside Paris, but just too elusive to imitate successfully. Today that luxury is more accessible, but it still retains its seductive appeal and charm. Paris is still the epitome of luxury.

Mademoiselle Chanel in 1935

these quality trades together) makes interesting reading. Especially interesting are the dates when certain companies were founded: Révillon, 1723; Baccarat, 1764; Château d'Yquem, 1786; Puiforcat, 1820; Hermès, 1837;

Boucheron, 1858; Bernardaud, 1863; Lanvin, 1889; Lalique, 1910. Quality has a long life and can be found in many industries, from fashion to silverware, from jewellery to perfume, from decoration to crystalware.

THE PRICE OF LUXURY ITEMS

Certain names still have the power to make people dream, and some dreams only come true if you can afford to pay for them. The price of luxury is relative, however. It's a question of authenticity, of the best materials, of exclusivity, of respect for the craftsman's skill. Christian Dior used to say that no price is too high to pay for quality. The famous *Kelly* bag by Hermès requires 18 hours of work and uses the finest quality leathers. It costs about 14,000F, but lasts a lifetime. A pure crystal Baccarat glass, handmade by a master craftsman, costs about 400F, but it's a genuine collector's item.

THE CAPITAL OF LUXURY

In France, luxury is often associated with its regional origins, but although silk comes from Lyon, perfumes from just outside Paris, silverware from Normandy and porcelain from Limoges, Paris is still the showcase. It's where it all happens, where everything is created and sold, often to a foreign clientele. The brochure produced by the Comité Colbert (a body which brings

WHO OWNS WHOM?

Most firms making luxury goods are still French-owned, saved by buyouts or by restructuring.

QUALITY AND LUXURY: HOW TO HANDLE IT

Parisian luxury need not be viewed from a distance. Push open the door of a great fashion house and step right into a dream world of elegance and refinement. At Dior, you can walk around as you please, from one showcase to the next. The well-trained sales staff are discreet, and you needn't be intimidated by their uniform (blue or black, depending on the store). Don't be afraid to look around at Hermès either. There's no obligation to buy and you'll see plenty of Japanese, who are not at all uncomfortable in the lovely surroundings.

The Puiforcat silversmiths and the Saint-Louis crystal works now belong to Hermès. The Wertheimer family have owned Chanel since 1924, and the LVMH group own Christian Dior, Givenchy, Christian Lacroix, Vuitton, Moët & Chandon, Hennessy and Kenzo. Cardin owns his own brand name and its many licences. The Sanofi group includes Yves Saint Laurent, Nina Ricci, and Roger & Gallet. As for the top

hotels, the situation is different. The Crillon is French, but the Ritz is Middle-Eastern owned, the Plaza and the George V are American and the Bristol is German.

WHO ARE THE BUYERS?

Apart from haute couture, luxury products have become gradually more accessible. Licences, franchises and company policies have helped to diversify and multiply the products. With the advent of advertising, famous names have became household words, giving products a wider popular appeal. Most couture houses have ready-to-wear collections (*prêt-à-porter*) (with names like *Bis, Parallèle, Bazar* and *Diffusion*) which are sold at competitive prices, but the style and quality are still maintained. Manufacturers of silver, porcelain and crystal always include less expensive items in their collections and constantly adapt them to suit changing tastes.

WHERE IT ALL HAPPENS

Every capital, from New York to Tokyo, from London to Milan,

has its own upmarket shopping district, where prestigious stores tend to group together. Do a spot of window shopping in Avenue Montaigne, Faubourg Saint-Honoré, Rue François-Ier, Rue Royale and Place Vendôme, streets which are synonymous with luxury. In recent years, Saint-Germain-des-Prés has also seen an influx of quality stores. Armani, Lacroix, Vuitton and de Castelbajac have joined Yves Saint Laurent at the Place Saint-Sulpice, thereby attracting a Left Bank (*rive gauche*) clientele that sometimes rather snobbily prefers to leave the Right Bank (*rive droite*) to the tourists.

PARISIAN DEPARTMENT STORES

AU BON MARCHÉ
PARIS

You could describe Paris as one large department store. In the Middle Ages, various trade associations grouped together in guilds set up their stalls in particular districts according to their products. This tradition continues today to a large extent, with specialist shops giving a particular character to different areas of the capital.

WHERE TO BUY WHAT

In the shop windows of the Avenue de la Grande-Armeé, you will see gleaming cars and cycles. Rue de Paradis boasts fine crystal and porcelain, while in Saint-Germain-des-Près and Odéon, you can enjoy browsing through bookshops or discover where the many publishing houses are situated. Faubourg

Saint-Antone is the place for furniture, sometimes a little flamboyant, and if you're looking for musical instruments or sheet music, head for the Rue de Rome. The more avant-garde fashion designers have set up shop in the Place des Victoires, whereas the main jewellers have

gathered in the Rue de la Paix and the Place Vendôme. Around the Marché Saint-Pierre, near the Sacré-Coeur, are the fabric shops, and the *prêt-à-porter* collections are mostly in the Sentier district, not far from where the national papers used to be based. Everything you could possibly want for your motorbike can be purchased near the Place de la Bastille, but if you are looking for computers, make your way to the Avenue Daumesnil, near the Gare de Lyon railway station.

THE HISTORY OF THE DEPARTMENT STORE

Most of the department stores in Paris are now over a hundred years old. Visiting them is rather like visiting a historic monument, but without the entrance fee. The first of its kind and still the most chic, Au Bon Marché was

founded in 1852 by Aristide Boucicaut and immortalised in a novel by Emile Zola called *Au Bonheur des Dames*. Au Printemps was founded by an ex-employee, Jules Jaluzot, on the Right Bank in 1865. La

Samaritaine was started in 1870 by Ernest Cognacq, a street vendor who sold ties on the Pont-Neuf. It is now the biggest department store in

16m/53ft high and 20m/66ft in diameter. Galeries Lafayette also has an extraordinary double dome, which is beautiful in the sunlight. The various buildings of La Samaritaine make up a fascinating history of commercial architecture from 1900 to 1930. Shop no. 2, near the Seine, has the most beautiful Art Deco-style façade in the capital. It was built in 1928 by Frantz Jourdain and Henri Sauvage. In 1932, shop no. 3 (on the corner of the Rue de Rivoli and Rue Boucher) was reconstructed in prefabricated materials in just six months, during which time

customers continued to shop inside it. The interior staircase was recently renovated by Andrée Putman.

Paris with a great view of the Seine from its restaurant. The 'newest' store is the Galeries Lafayette, founded in 1899 by Alphonse Kahn and Theophile Bader.

SPECIALIST STORES
Even though they stock similar merchandise, the Parisian department stores often have their individual strong points. The Bazar de l'Hôtel de Ville (BHV) is a mecca for do-it-yourself enthusiasts. La Samaritaine is famous for its hardware and gardening departments and its work wear. Au Printemps has a 'Boutique Blanche' which is very popular for wedding lists. Au Bon Marché is a very smart and classic store, with an excellent food hall which is a popular spot for those living on the Left Bank whilst Galeries Lafayette is better-known for fashion

items (especially clothes, but also perfumes and accessories). The department stores need to keep their customers' loyalty and interest, so they often organise exhibitions around a theme (China, Vietnam, England), which are usually very good. The culture of a country is explained with typical products, arts and crafts, traditional clothes and antique furniture. Whether or not you intend to buy, these events are certinly worth a visit.

ARCHITECTURE
Au Bon Marché was built by Gustave Eiffel, and recently renovated by Andrée Putman, who designed the unusual central escalator. Au Printemps is like an enormous ocean liner. It has a huge glass dome, dating from 1923, which is

ADDRESSES
■ AU BON MARCHÉ
22, Rue de Sèvres, 75007.
■ PRINTEMPS
64, Blvd Haussmann, 75009.
■ GALERIES LAFAYETTE
40, Blvd Haussmann, 75009.
■ LA SAMARITAINE
19, Rue de la Monnaie, 75001.
■ BHV
52, Rue de Rivoli, 75004.

Paris – practicalities

W ith more than 2,100,000 people living in 39 square miles (100 square kilometres), divided into 20 *arrondissements,* Paris is simply too large to visit in a single day.

GETTING AROUND THE CITY

BY METRO

The underground system is the fastest and easiest way to get around Paris. The maps are clear and well-marked, and there is almost always a station within a few blocks of where you want to go. With 15 different lines and many transfer stations, the metro system covers Paris like an underground spider's web.

The metro is open from 5.30am-12.30am. A single ticket is valid for any destination within the city limits. A ticket costs 8F, but it is more economical to purchase a *carnet* of 10 tickets for 55F. They can be purchased in the metro, in tobacco shops *(tabacs)* and tourist offices.

Metro passes are economical as they allow an unlimited number of trips. These include the one-day *Mobilis* (30F), and the one-, two-, three- or five-day *Paris Visite* (50-170F), with the added advantage of a 25-35% discount at certain Paris monuments and museums.

BY BUS

This is a good way to actually see the city, but not if you get stuck in a Paris traffic jam! There are 59 bus lines, plus the PC *(petite ceinture)*, which travels around the edge of Paris via the ringroad. Buses run from 7am- 8.30pm or 12.30am, depending on the lines. Unfortunately, many lines do not run on Sundays or holidays. A late-night bus system, called the *Noctambus,* includes 18 lines that run every hour, 1am-5.30am. The ticket costs 30F regardless of the destination and transfers are allowed.

The bus is free with a *Mobilis* or *Paris Visite* pass. Free maps are available at the métro ticket counters.

For a comfortable way to see Paris, take the *Balabus.* Operated by the RATP, it runs on Sundays and holidays from April to September, from 12.30pm-8pm.

> OFFICES
> OF THE RATP
> **Place de la Madeleine**
> You can get all the information you need at this office. Or try calling for information in English:
> ☎ 08 36 68 41 14

The 90 min trip takes you from the Gare de Lyon to the Grande Arche de la Défense, and passes all the major monuments in the capital.

BY TAXI

Taxis can be hailed on the street or at one of the taxi stations marked with a large sign. The meter starts running with an initial fare of about 13F. The rates go up after 7pm and outside the city limits; there is also an extra charge for pickups of about 13F if you telephone for a taxi, and for luggage (6F per suitcase). Taxi-drivers generally expect cash and a 10%t tip. A taxi is available if the light on the top is lit up (it is occupied when just a small bulb is on). Taxis can refuse you if your group has more than three people or an animal. Paris has a number of radio-dispatched taxi firms, including:

Taxis Bleus
☎ 01 49 36 10 10

G7
☎ 01 47 39 47 39

Taxis 7000
☎ 01 42 70 00 42

See p. 116 for further taxi information

BY CAR

Driving in Paris is not exactly relaxing if you're not used to the traffic and don't know your way around. Not to mention the challenge of finding a parking spot. Traffic wardens, who once wore easy-to-spot light blue uniforms, now patrol the streets in discreet navy blue. And they are quick to write out tickets (from 75 to 220F apiece!). Although some streets forbid parking altogether, most allow pay parking, where you purchase a ticket from one of the meters on the street and park from 1 to 2 hours.

Underground parking areas also exist, but are fairly expensive.

Consider yourself forewarned: cars do get impounded in Paris. If you come out of a museum or café and can't find your car, it may have been towed away (call ☎ 01 55 76 20 80). One last tip, buy a good map before you leave or first thing when you arrive.

You can get fuel 24 hours a day at: Mobil, 151, Rue de la Convention, 75015; or Total, George-V car park, 75008.

BY BIKE

Two years ago, with the municipal elections coming up, the city government created a series of lanes and streets reserved for bicycles (the quays along the Seine, for example, are closed to traffic on Sundays during the summer months). Bicycles are a great way to see the city, but be careful, cars won't make it easy for you. Depending on the weather conditions, the pollution levels can be fairly high on certain days. Some cyclists in Paris choose to wear masks. Bike rentals:

Paris à vélo c'est sympa,
☎ 01 48 87 60 01
Paris-Vélo,
☎ 01 43 37 59 22.

BY TOUR BUS

You can 'do' Paris by bus in just a few hours.
Cityrama
4, pl. des Pyramides, 75001
☎ 01 44 55 60 00
Paris-Vision
214, rue de Rivoli, 75001
☎ 01 42 60 31 25.

WRITING HOME

Stamps are available at post offices (closed Sunday and Saturday after 12pm) and at tobacco shops (*le tabac*). Yellow letterboxes are easily found on the streets (last pickup is around 6 or 7pm at the post offices and from 8 to 10pm at the main post office located on the Rue du Louvre). Outgoing mail can also be left at the reception desk of your hotel.

The main post office (52, Rue du Louvre, 75001, ☎ 01 40 28 20 00) is open 24 hours a day if you need to make a phone call or buy a stamp when the other offices are closed.

MAKING A TELEPHONE CALL

You can use one of the many public telephone booths located throughout Paris to catch up with the folks back home (it will be less expensive than a hotel phone). You will need a phonecard (*Telecarte*), which can be purchased at a post office or tobacco shop (*le tabac*).

CHANGING MONEY

Foreign currency can be exchanged at banks (closed Sunday and usually Saturday) and bureaux de change. Small bureaux de change are often open on Sundays in popular tourist areas: for example, at 1, Rue Hautefeuille, 75006, ☎ 01 46 34 70 46 or Thomas Cook, 8, Pl. de l'Opéra, 75009 ☎ 01 47 42 46 52.

OPENING HOURS

Most museums and monuments are open from 10am to 8pm six days a week (except for certain holidays). Smaller museums may close during lunch hours, so it's wise to call ahead. National museums are closed on Tuesday; city of Paris museums are closed on Monday.

The *Musées et Monuments* pass is a good way to explore Paris; it is good for unlimited access to 70 museums and monuments in Paris and the surrounding region and allows you to skip the queues. A one-day pass costs 80F; a three-day pass 160F, and a five-day pass 240F. You can purchase them at the monuments and museums themselves, or at the tourist office.

If you're short on time, *Paristoric*, a 45-minute big-screen show is an excellent introduction to the history of Paris. Shows run every hour, from 9am-9pm.

Paristoric:
11 bis Rue Scribe, 75009
☎ 01 42 66 62 06.

You have to try everything at least once, including a *Bateaux-Mouches* trip on the Seine. It's ideal in good weather or for a romantic candle-lit dinner for two,

in the company of Paris' most beautiful sights.

Vedettes du Pont-Neuf
Square du Vert-Galant
☎ 01 46 33 98 38

Bateaux du pont de l'Alma
Right Bank
☎ 01 42 25 96 10

Bateaux Parisiens, at the base of the Eiffel Tower
☎ 01 44 11 33 55.

The Eiffel Tower and Trocadéro

One of the best views of Paris is from Trocadéro, looking past the Eiffel Tower to the Champs de Mars and the École Militaire. This setting was created for the Universal Exhibition of 1889 and 1937. In the summer, cafés set up tables outdoors, while skateboarders and rollerskaters whizz around the marble-lined terraces of the Chaillot Palace with their walkmans and ghetto blasters.

③ **Guimet Museum**

PLACE D'IÉNA

Wilson

④ **Museum of Modern Art**

⑤ Avenue du Président

PLACE DU TROCADÉRO ⑦

Av. Albert de Mun ⑥

Chaillot Palace ②

New York

Seine

PONT

D'IÉNA

Eiffel Tower ①

This old lady of iron, constructed to celebrate the centennial of the French Revolution, carries her years with amazing grace and style. With 6 million visitors every year, it is one of the most-visited monuments in Paris. You can walk up or take the lift to the upper platforms. There are shops, restaurants, lookouts, and one of the best views of Paris from nearly 300m/1,000 ft high. On a clear day, you can see for 90kms/55 miles.

❶ The Eiffel Tower (Tour Eiffel) ★★★
Champ-de-Mars, 75007.
☎ 01 44 11 23 23
Open every day 9.30am-11pm (mid-June to Aug. 24 hours a day). Entry charge.

❷ The Chaillot Palace (Palais de Chaillot) ★★★
17, Pl. du Trocadéro, 75016.

Built for the 1937 Universal Exhibition, Chaillot houses

museums, a theatre, a film library and restaurants.

Theatre Chaillot
☎ 01 53 65 31 00

Musee de l'Homme
☎ 01 44 05 72 72
Open every day (exc. Tue.), 9.45am-5.15pm. Entry charge.

This museum traces human evolution through archaeology, ethnology and anthropology.

Musee de la Marine
☎ 01 53 65 69 69
Open every day (exc. Tue.), 10am-6pm. Entry charge.

The story of the French navy is told through a series of models, making it a perfect place to take children.

Le Totem
☎ 01 47 27 28 29
Open every day noon-2.30pm, 7.30pm-midnight.

This restaurant in the Musée de l'Homme has a great view of the Eiffel Tower and Trocadéro Gardens, with ornamental pool, sculptures and fountains.

It is spectacular at night, when the fountains and palace are illuminated.

❸ Guimet Museum (Musée Guimet) ★★★
19, Ave. d'Iena, 75106
☎ 01 45 05 00 98
Open every day (exc. Tue.), 9.45am-6pm (last adm. 4.45pm). Entry charge.

This is one of world's leading museums of Asian art, housing an excellent collection of Cambodian (Khmer) pieces, including temple sculptures and Buddhist statues from Japan, India, Vietnam and Indonesia.

❹ The Museum of Modern Art of the City of Paris (Musée d'Art Moderne) ★★★

11, Ave. du President-Wilson, 75016.
☎ 01 40 70 11 10 (recording).
Open Tue.-Sun, 10am-5.30pm (Sat.-Sun., 10am-6.45pm). Entry charge.

You'll find works by Vuillard, Picasso, Modigliani, van Dogen, Dufy and Bonnard in this collection. *The Dance* by Matisse is a highlight of the museum, which also has a shop, bookshop and cafeteria with a terrace for sunny days.

❺ Carette ★★
4, Pl. du Trocadéro, 75016
☎ 01 47 27 88 56
Open every day, 8am-7pm (closed Aug.).

This restaurant has a charmingly old-fashioned decor, and it's as famous for its macaroons as for its lovely terrace. Parisians come here to see and be seen, and the odd lost tourist sometimes seeks sustenance here too.

❼ A QUICK STROLL IN THE 16TH DISTRICT ★★

Leave the Place du Trocadéro by the Rue Benjamin Franklin (off the right wing of the Chaillot Palace), and stroll towards Passy and Auteuil. At no. 47 on the very pretty Rue Raynouard, Balzac wrote many of his famous novels. It's open Tue.-Sun., 10am-5.15pm, and has an entry charge. To your right is the Maison de Radio France. Continue along the Rue la Fontaine, which has some lovely Art Nouveau bow windows and wrought-iron railings.

❻ Cinémathèque Francaise ★★
7, Ave. Albert de Mun, 75016
☎ 01 56 26 01 01 (recording)
Screenings Wed.-Sun., 7pm & 9pm.

40,000 films are housed in the archive of this film library, which are restored and shown to the public. Many are classics, and visitors can enjoy rare retrospective gems. If you're a film buff, don't miss it. The programme is published in *Pariscope* or the *Officiel des Spectacles*.

The Champs-Élysées

The Champs-Élysées has a new look, all the cars parked along the pavements have gone, and rows of trees have been planted in their place. Crowds pour out of every metro station at the weekend to enjoy the fast-food restaurants, cinemas and shopping arcades. Strangely enough, Saturday mornings are different, and the avenue is calm, with the empty cafés offering quiet havens from which to enjoy the majestic view.

the Arc is early in the day, when morning light emphasizes the details of the sculpture. The view from the top is magnificent.

❷ Prunier Traktir ★★
16, Ave. Victor-Hugo, 75016
☎ 01 44 17 35 85
Open Mon.-Sat., noon-11pm,
(closed mid-June- mid-Aug.).

This is an architectural jewel from the 1920s. The glass façade alone is worth the trip, as is the restaurant, with its decor of black marble, mahogany, gold leaf and mosaics. This was one of the Windsors' favourite haunts when they were in Paris. Sit at the bar and order a seafood platter or oysters.

❸ The Champs-Élysées ★★★
In the late 17th century, the Champs Élysées was nothing more than an empty field,

❶ Arc de Triomphe ★★★
Place du Général-de-Gaulle, 75008
☎ 01 55 37 73 77
Open every day April-Sept., 9.30am-11pm, Oct.-March 10am-10pm. Entry charge.

Chalgrin drew up the plans for the Arc for Napoleon I, who wanted a monument worthy of his great army. Fate decided otherwise, and the work was not entirely completed until 1836, during the reign of Louis-Philippe. The best time to see

before Le Nôtre planted it with trees to extend the royal view from the Tuileries. During the Second Empire, a constant stream of horse-drawn carriages paraded up the street, so that women could show off their outfits. 'The most beautiful street in

the world' has lost much of its sparkle today, but it's still a must for most visitors at some time during their stay.

The Champs-Élysées at the turn of the century

➍ Fouquet's ★★

99, Ave. des Champs-Élysées, 75008

☎ 01 47 23 70 60
Open every day 8am-2am.

Anyone who is anyone has come to this bar. Fouquet's elegant past is remembered with nostalgia. The terrace on the corner of the Avenue George V is still one of the most beautiful in Paris. The speciality is the 'César', the cocktail created by the bartender and dedicated to the famous French sculptor.

➎ Virgin Megastore★

52, Ave. des Champs-Élysées, 75008
☎ 01 49 53 50 00
Open Mon.-Sat., 10am-midnight, Sun. and hol., noon-midnight.

Virgin transformed a temple of money into a temple of music. The lovely marble architecture of the 1930s building, the former offices of the National City Bank of New York, was left untouched. Several thousand people come here every day to explore the multimedia, Internet, television, hi-fi, video, CD and cassette departments. There is also a bookshop and ticket office.

➏ Planet Hollywood ★

78, Ave. des Champs-Élysées, 75008
☎ 01 53 83 78 27
Open every day 11am-1am.

The staircase is lined with hand prints of Hollywood stars, while clothes and memorabilia from American blockbusters decorate the interior. The restaurant belongs to Sylvester Stallone, Arnold Schwarzenegger and Bruce Willis, among others.

THE SHOPPING ARCADES ON THE CHAMPS-ÉLYSÉES

You can find everything from a teddy bear to a model of the Eiffel Tower in these arcades, but the chic shops of the Galerie des Champs, Arcades du Lido, Galerie Point-Show and Galerie Élysées-La Boétie are rather expensive and often uncomfortably crowded with tourists.

The food is Tex-Mex or American. Kids love it, but it's crowded at lunch and dinner times and on Saturday nights.

Madeleine – Rue Saint-Honoré

The neighbourhood around the classically styled Madeleine church starts buzzing very early. Tourists do their shopping along the Rue Royale and the Faubourg Saint-Honoré, in luxury shops such as Hermès, Lalique and Christofle. Jewellery, crystal and porcelain boutiques line the streets of this district, along with the more recent interior design shops, where you'll discover the latest in furniture and fabrics. Have a good look around, even if you don't buy, it's always fun.

❶ Madeleine Church (Église de la Madeleine) ★★★
Open every day 7am-1.30pm and 3.30pm-7pm.

After many delays, it was the architect Vignon who finally designed this solid church based on a Greek temple.

The style of the interior (1830-1840) is extremely lavish. On your way out, stop at the top of the steps to enjoy a magnificent view down the Rue Royale towards the Place de la Concorde.

❷ Despalles ★★★
Village Royal, 26, Rue Boissy-d'Anglas, 75008
☎ 01 49 24 05 65
Open Mon.-Sat.,10am-7pm.

A shop for town and country. On one side there's a vast expanse of plants, garden furniture and outdoor items for terraces and gardens and

on the other, an interior design shop, with furniture and gifts. In keeping with the district they are both chic and pricey.

❸ Hédiard ★★
21, Pl. de la Madeleine, 75008
☎ 01 43 12 88 88
Open Mon.-Sat. 9.30am-9pm (delicatessen) to 11pm (wine cellar).

Step inside and you'll be transported by the smells, colours and flavours. Hédiard has renovated the shop completely and customers can enjoy a taste of the exotic. The tearoom upstairs is decorated in a style that hovers somewhere between a transatlantic liner and a café in the twenties.

❹ Hermès ★★★
24, Rue du Faubourg Saint-Honoré, 75008
☎ 01 40 17 47 17
Open Mon. 10am-1pm, 2.15-6.30pm, Tues.-Sat. 10am-6.30pm.

Everything at Hermès is a visual delight, starting with the stunning window displays. Make sure you see all the different departments, where you'll find saddles, leather goods, clothes and jewellery. The choice of bags and scarves is superb, but a Hermès scarf will set you back 1390F, though you could content yourself with an elegant deck of cards, a snip at just 200F.

❺ Hotel Crillon ★★
10, Place de la Concorde, 75008
☎ 01 44 71 15 00

This hotel has a wonderful location and offers the height of elegance. Don't be frightened to pop in between 3.30-7pm, when you can listen to the very talented harpist in the Winter Garden Tearooms and enjoy a cup of tea or coffee for 30FF.

HÔTEL DE CRILLON
PARIS

❻ Bernardaud Tearoom ★★
Galerie Royale, 9, Rue Royale, 75008
☎ 01 42 66 22 55
Open Mon.-Fri. 8.30am-7pm, Sat., 12-7pm.

Come here to escape the noise of the city. The walls are a soothing pale green colour, like Japanese green-tea ice-cream. Bernardaud's fine porcelain pieces are displayed in the alcoves, and when you select your tea, you can also choose the colour and style of the cup in which it's served. You'll emerge refreshed and ready for the pace of Paris again.

❼ Territoire ★★★
30, Rue Boissy-d'Anglas, 75008
☎ 01 42 66 22 13
Open Mon.-Sat. 10.30am-7pm (closed Aug.).

SHOWCASE OF PARISIAN LUXURY

Along with the Avenue Montaigne, this district represents the height of luxury. Here you'll find many of the well known Italian names, including Gucci, Versace and Cerruti, and the big American designers, still led by Ralph Lauren. The arcades, shop windows and even the Madeleine church have all been renovated. At Christmas the decorations are stunning.

The former Hotel de Lully is a heritage building, with a wooden façade. It is a real treasure trove, where you could find just about

anything, including books, clothes, games, stationery, plates and wicker baskets such as your grandmother may have had. It's a great place to spend an hour or two.

The Palais-Royal

Step through the gates of the Palais-Royal and the noise and bustle of the city disappear as if by magic. The garden and arcades, where seditious pamphlets circulated and the Revolution began, offer a welcome haven. Shops have lined the garden since the 18th century, but the stamp dealers and shops selling miniature lead soldiers have since been replaced by fashion and interior design boutiques. However, there's still a restaurant or two for lunch or an afternoon coffee.

❷ À Marie Stuart ★
3, 4, 5, Galerie de Montpensier, 75001
☎ **01 42 96 28 25**
Open Mon.-Fri. 9am-6.30pm, Sat. 9am-12.30pm & 2-5.30pm.

A wonderful but tiny shop with a 19th century varnished wooden counter, where customers once came for funeral items made from jet and black onyx. It's now a good place to find military medals and badges.

❶ Palais-Royal ★★★
Pl. du Palais-Royal, 75001.

Richelieu constructed this architectural complex in 1636. Louis XIV then gave it to his brother, the Duke of Orleans, in 1692. In the 18th century, the architect Louis designed the arcades we see today. They were subsequently sold to shopowners, but then gambling houses and late-night cafés also moved in, becoming the favourite haunt of prostitutes and political rabble-rousers.

❸ Maison de Vacances ★★

63-64, Galerie de
Montpensier, 75001
☎ 01 47 03 99 74
Open Mon. 1-7pm, Tue.-Fri.
11am-7pm. Closed Sat. in
summer

Everything is crisp and fresh
in this shop, which specialises

in table and household linen.
You'll find embroidered and
openwork linen and lace
trompe-l'œil painted on wall
mirrors. They also sell wool
and cashmere cushions for
around 500F.

❹ Didier Ludot ★★

20, 24, Galerie de
Montpensier, 75001
☎ 01 42 96 06 56
Open Mon.-Sat. 10.30am-7pm.

Don't miss this shop. Didier
Ludot tracks down haute-
couture clothes and
accessories, which he then
sells for 50% of the original
price. Top brand names
include Chanel, Dior,
Balmain, Balenciaga and
Hermès. Buy your Kelly bag
and accessories here.

❺ L'Escalier d'Argent ★★

42, Galerie de Montpensier,
75001
☎ 01 40 20 05 33
Open Tue.-Sat. 1-7pm.

This antique dealer has a
passion for the 18th century,
reflected in her handmade
waistcoats (starting at
1,400F). She uses precious
silks, velvets and brocades,
together with period or
reproduction fabrics to create
these fabulous items.

❻ Les Salons du Palais-Royal Shiseido ★★★

142, Galerie de Valois,
75001
☎ 01 49 27 09 09
Open Mon.-Sat. 9am-7pm.

Serge Lutens uses a purple
and violet backdrop for the
exclusive perfumes from
Shiseido. Panels painted
with 18th century designs,
with a frieze of insects, suns
and moons, surround a spiral
staircase with bronze fittings.
It's worth popping in just for
a look at the decoration.

❼ Muriel Grateau ★★

130, 133, Galerie de Valois,
75001
☎ 01 40 20 90 30
Open Mon. 2-7pm, Tue.-Sat.
11am-1pm & 1.30-7pm.

This is one of the most
sophisticated design shops in
Paris. You'll find plain or

damask linens in every pastel
shade you can imagine,
displayed on wrought-iron
furniture. Accessories for the
table, bedroom and bathroom
are available, plus tablecloths
and mats to match a selection
of glasses, plates and serving
dishes.

Place des Victoires

The balance and the symmetry of the 17th-century architecture create a perfect showcase for the designer boutiques that have moved into buildings, originally designed by Hardouin-Mansart, the architect of Versailles. Kenzo, Cacharel, Esprit, Victoire, Mugler and Kelian have found their location perfect. The centrepiece is a statue of Louis XIV, erected in 1822 to replace the original destroyed in the Revolution. The *Place des Victoires* and the nearby streets are a must for shoppers. It's also a favourite spot for journalists and designers, but in the early evening it begins to calm down.

Map labels: Notre-Dame-des-Victoires; R. Vivienne; Galerie; R. de la Banque; N.D. des Victoires; R. des Petits-Champs; R. de Beaujolais; Jardin du Palais Royal; Rue de Valois; R. des Petits; R. la Feuillade; PLACE DES PETITS-PÈRES; PLACE DES VICTOIRES; R. la Vrillère; R. E. Marcel; R. d'Argout; R. Hérold; R. Coquillière; Rue du Petits-Champs; des Colonel Driant; Rue Croix des Petits-Champs; Galerie Véro-Dodat; du Boulois

by the Galerie du Passage, Capia, Il Bisonte, and Eric Philippe. Then take a break at the Époque café.

❷ Anna Joliet, Music Boxes ★★

9, Rue de Beaujolais, 75001
☎ 01 42 96 55 13
Open Mon.-Sat. 10am-7pm,
(Aug. 1-7pm).

❶ La Galerie Véro-Dodat ★★★

19, Rue Jean-Jacques-Rousseau, 75001.

The only thing that's disappeared here over the years is the original owner. Everything else, including the black-and-white tiled floor, the curved windows with copper frames and mirrored pilasters, is still in place. Look at the window displays as you stroll

This tiny shop in the former home of the writer Colette is worth seeing even if you aren't a specialist. Melodies from hundreds of different music boxes (both for children and collectors) fill the air. Prices for music boxes start at 200F.

❸ NOTRE-DAME DES VICTOIRES

Notre-Dame des Victoires reflected the piety of the common people, as shown by the moving commemorative plaques that cover the walls and pillars. Built to honour the saviour of La Rochelle from the Protestants, the church was completed in 1740. During the Revolution, it was used as a commodities exchange.

❹ La Galerie Vivienne ★★★
4, Rue des Petits-Champs, 75001.

Some of the boutiques lining the glass-roofed arcade have remained unchanged since the 19th century, when they first opened, relics of a Paris long since disappeared. You'll see vases by Emilio Robba, petit-point pillows and rugs at the Casa Lopez, unusual furniture by Christian Astuguevieille, sunglasses at Cutler & Gross and many other designer boutiques.

❺ Peter Hadley ★★
6 bis, Pl. des Petits-Pères, 75001
☎ 01 42 86 83 73
Open Mon.-Sat., 10am-7pm.

The shopfront, and the name, 'La Maison Bleue', painted over the door of this shop opposite the Notre-Dame des Victoires church, still remain. The religious objects have disappeared however, now replaced by chic sportswear designed for adventurous outdoor pursuits.

❻ Ventilo ★★
27 bis, Rue du Louvre, 75001
☎ 01 42 33 18 67
Open Mon.-Sat. 10.30am-7.30pm. Closed Aug.

There are three floors to explore in this shop. On one floor you'll discover women's fashions in natural, flowing fabrics and styles, and on another, quilts from Provence, cushions, lamps and perfumes. Exhausted, you can flop into a lavender or honey-coloured cane armchair in the tearoom.

❼ A Priori Thé ★★
35, Galerie Vivienne, 75001
☎ 01 42 97 48 75
Open Mon.-Fri. 9am-6pm, Sat. 9am-6.30pm, Sun. 12.30-6.30pm.

The charm of this tearoom is due mostly to its location, the lovely light on sunny days and its covered terrace. It is rather English in style but with

international staff and a menu which is a combination of both. Enjoy the brownies and crumbles at this favourite haunt of journalists and people from the world of fashion. It's a good spot to come with the family at the weekend.

The Louvre and the Tuileries

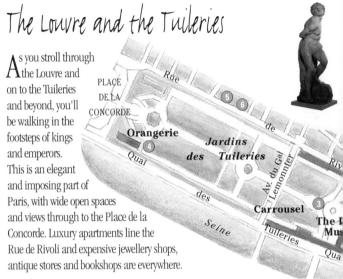

As you stroll through the Louvre and on to the Tuileries and beyond, you'll be walking in the footsteps of kings and emperors. This is an elegant and imposing part of Paris, with wide open spaces and views through to the Place de la Concorde. Luxury apartments line the Rue de Rivoli and expensive jewellery shops, antique stores and bookshops are everywhere.

❶ Louvre Museum (Musée du Louvre) ★★★

Métro: Palais-Royal-Musée du Louvre, enter through the Passage Richelieu
☎ 01 40 20 51 51
Open every day 9am-6pm, (exc. Tue.) (Wed. and Mon. to 9.45pm). Entry charge.

A week isn't long enough to see the entire museum, but if you can only make one trip, don't miss the newly fitted areas of the Grand Louvre: the Cour Marly and its 18th-century sculptures, the Cour Khorsabad, the Michelangelo Gallery, the former stables of Napoleon III and the fine medieval Italian sculpture.

❷ Café Marly ★★

93, Rue de Rivoli, Passage Richelieu, 75001
☎ 01 49 26 06 60
Open every day 8am-2am.

There's no better place to enjoy lunch than the Napoleon III rooms and gallery which overlook the illuminated glass pyramid. Renovated by Olivier Gagnère and Yves Taralon, it's one of the city's most chic meeting-places for brunch on Sundays.

❸ Carrousel du Louvre ★★

99, Rue de Rivoli, 75001
☎ 01 43 16 47 47

Shops open every day 9am-8pm (exc. Tue.). Restaurants open every day to 11pm.

Forty shops (all open on Sunday), restaurants and fast-food outlets are all here, including Lalique, the Virgin Megastore and Rooming. Try to visit Nature et Découverte, an environmentally friendly store for kids and adults, and the shop at the Postal Museum, where writing is still considered an art.

➍ Jardins des Tuileries ★★★

The gardens have recently been restored to their original 17th-century design by Le Nôtre and with 700 newly planted trees they will soon return to their former glory. Don't miss the Musée de l'Orangerie, near the Place de la Concorde: ☎ 01 42 97 48 16. Open Wed.-Mon. 9.45am-5.pm.

Louvre des Antiquaires

SOME UNMISSABLE PAINTINGS AT THE LOUVRE

Vermeer's *The Lacemaker* (c. 1665) is an exquisite painting portraying domestic life in Holland in the 17th century and Watteau's 'Gilles' is a nostalgic depiction of 18th-century gallantry. Also try to see the romantic works of Delacroix, full of heightened emotion, not to mention Georges de la Tour's *The cheat with the ace of diamonds* and of course the *Mona Lisa* (*La Joconde* in French, if you are looking for signs) by Leonardo da Vinci.

Claude Monet's superb water lily series, known as *Nympheas*, is housed here and you can see works by Modigliani, Renoir, Soutine and Rousseau, amongst others.

➎ Inter-Continental Hotel ★★
3, Rue de Castiglione, 75001
☎ 01 44 77 11 11.

Have a relaxing drink on the terrace of the 'Interconti', as it is known by the locals, after your tour of the Tuileries and the Louvre. Enjoy a coffee outside in the sun for 30F. It's ideally placed between the Tuileries and the Place Vendôme.

➏ Galignani ★★
224, Rue de Rivoli, 75001
☎ 01 42 60 76 07
Open Mon.-Sat. 10am-7pm.

Opened in 1802, the Galignani publishing company later transformed itself into a reading room where people could peruse foreign newspapers and publications, unavailable elsewhere. Today Galignani is just as welcoming, with its 1930s woodwork and long rows of books to rummage through. It's one of the great bookshops of Paris with a treasure trove of literary, lifestyle, art, painting and architectural publications.

➐ Louvre des Antiquaires ★★
2, Pl. du Palais-Royal, 75001.
☎ 01 42 97 27 00
Open Tue.-Sun. 11am-7pm, (closed Sun. in July & Aug.).

You'll probably pay top prices, but if you can't find what you want here, you probably won't find it anywhere. A group of small shops selling furniture, paintings, objets d'art and sculptures, with a jewellery market in the basement.

Faubourg Saint-Germain

This is an old and aristocratic area in the shadow of the Invalides, where the most beautiful houses are often hidden away in charming old courtyards full of greenery and flowers. The streets are calm and elegant, and dotted with cars ferrying ministers around Paris. The shopfronts blend tastefully with the 17th-and 18th-century façades though without these antique dealers, booksellers and interior decorators, much of the charm of this quarter would be lost.

❶ The Invalides ★★★
Place des Invalides, 75007
☎ **01 44 42 37 67**
Open every day 10am-5pm, to 6pm in summer. Entry charge.

The Classical façade, the main courtyard and the Saint-Louis de Libéral Bruand Church make this one of the architectural masterpieces of the 18th century. If uniforms are your weakness, don't miss the museum, which has one of the best collections in the world of arms and armour, each one of which is a work of art. Finish off your visit with Napoleon's tomb, which lies directly under the dome of Jules Hardouin-Mansart's church.

❷ The Orsay Museum (Musée d'Orsay) ★★★
Rue de Bellechasse, 75007.
☎ **01 40 49 48 14**
Open 10am-6pm, (Thur. to 10pm). Closed Mon. Entry charge.

This is Paris' temple of 19th century art and design. The

collection of Impressionist paintings is exceptional, and several masterpieces have recently been acquired by the museum, including Courbet's *Origin of the World,* until now hidden in private collections, *Starry Night* by Van Gogh, Renoir's *Reclining Nude* and

❸ 'LE CARRÉ RIVE GAUCHE'

The cream of the Paris antique dealers are located within an area bordered by the Quai Voltaire, the Rue des Saints-Pères, the Rue de l'Université and the Rue du Bac. The furniture, objects and paintings are often of exceptional quality. The Carré exhibits its masterpieces in May, and anyone who is anyone comes to have a look.

his *Portrait of Fernand Halphen*. There is also and a mahogany writing desk by Henry van de Velde. Don't forget the tearoom, restaurant, bookshop, and a museum shop with reproductions of the paintings.

❹ The Maillol Museum (Musée Maillol) ★★★

61, Rue de Grenelle, 75007
☎ 01 42 22 59 58
Open every day 11am-6pm. (exc. Tue. & holidays).

The former Bouchardon *hôtel*, where Musset once lived, now houses the collection of Dina Vierny, Maillol's last model.

It includes lesser-known aspects of the artist's work, including paintings and tapestries. His pastels and chalk sketches are masterpieces.

❺ Siècle ★★

24, Rue du Bac, 75007
☎ 01 47 03 48 03
Open Mon. to Sat. 10.30am-7pm.

Here, each object is treated as if it were unique – and it often is. Ornate designs decorate the silverware, the glasses have curvacious stems shaped like a body and the plates take you back to the elegance of centuries past and long forgotten.

❻ Au Nom de la Rose ★★

46, Rue du Bac, 75007
☎ 01 42 22 08 09
Open Mon.- Sat. 9am-9pm.

This sunny boutique is brimming with rose petals. They're on the linen, the pillows, the scarves and the jewellery. You can buy rose-scented candles, candied rose petals (from 45F) and, behind a wrought-iron doorway, you'll find the garden – filled with old roses.

❼ Bonpoint ★★

86, Rue de l'Université, 75007
☎ 01 45 51 46 28
Open Mon.-Sat. 10am-7pm.

The refurbished Bonpoint shop now has a contemporary feel. Small useful gifts, wrapped in embroidered linen

pouches, are slipped in between the clothes in linen-covered baskets. The fashion boutique is at 67, Rue de l'Université (☎ 01 45 51 53 18). Try on the outfits in linen, silk and velvet in the lovely fitting rooms decorated with a wrought-iron and crystal chandelier.

❽ Les Nuits d'Été ★★

22, Rue de Beaune, 75007
☎ 01 47 03 92 07
Open every day noon-7pm. Closed Sun. in June & July. Closed Aug.

This is a discreet and cosy meeting place for locals and editors from the nearby publishing houses. Friendly and hospitable, it's a good venue for Sunday brunch.

Saint-Germain-des-Prés

Just the words 'Saint-Germain-des-Prés' are capable of conjuring up a fascinating era, recalling such colourful and bohemian characters as Jean-Paul Sartre and Simone de Beauvoir at the Café de Flore, Boris Vian at the Tabou and Hemingway at the Deux Magots. The streets are full of the past, and it's a perfect area in which to wander, past galleries and antique dealers, shops, restaurants and nightclubs and then to relax in a café, from where you can watch the world go by.

and the beautiful Baroque building was given over to it in 1805. Its curved wings overlooking the Seine give it a rather Roman appearance .

❶ The Institute of France ★★★
23, Quai de Conti, 75006
Closed to the public.

The Palais de l'Institute is home to the illustrious Académie Française, who meet under the cupola designed by Louis le Vau, this building was constructed as a palace in 1688. Cardinal Richelieu founded the academy in 1635,

❷ Shu Uemura ★★
176, Blvd Saint-Germain, 75006
☎ 01 45 48 02 55
Open Mon. 11am-7pm,
Tue. -Sat. 10am-7pm.

With over 100 different shades of make-up, lipstick, eyeshadow and blusher, this shop this is a veritable temple to the art of *maquillage*

(make-up). Beauticians make up one side of your face, you finish off the other side and carry home a sketch describing how to do it all by yourself. It's practical and fun.

❸ Triff Gallery ★★
35, Rue Jacob, 75006
☎ 01 42 60 22 60
Open Mon. 2.30-7pm, Tue.-Sat. 10.30am-7pm.

Take a trip to the Middle East starting at the end of a tree-lined avenue in Paris. The carpets are strewn around the floor in colourful chaos. A fountain in the middle of the gallery makes you feel as if you're in a Syrian palace. Just the decor itself is worth the trip, not to mention the kilims, and old books and fabrics.

❹ Au Fond de la Cour ★★
49, Rue de Seine, 75006
☎ 01 43 25 81 89
Open Mon.-Sat. 11am-7pm.

This boutique overflows into the courtyard, where the rattan and wrought-iron

furniture have an attractive sheen. Inside, the shop looks like one of Napoleon III's greenhouses, with curios, lamps, chandeliers decorated with flowers and foliage and a gallery of mirrors. A lovely place to browse, even if you leave empty-handed.

❺ La Palette ★★
43, Rue de Seine, 75006
☎ 01 43 26 68 15
Open Mon.-Sat. 8am-2am.

This café could not be in any other city. Come rain or shine, summer or winter, the tables are out on the pavement. Enjoy a glass of wine in the company of artists, models and actors. La Palette is a local institution. Without it, Saint-Germain just wouldn't be the same.

❻ Cafés along Boulevard Saint-Germain ★★★
At 172:
LE CAFÉ DE FLORE
☎ 01 45 48 55 26
Open every day 7am-1.30am.
At 170:
LES DEUX MAGOTS
☎ 01 45 48 55 25
Open every day 7.30am-2am.

It's too hard to choose, so try them both. Early in the morning, a breakfast at the

❼ FURSTENBERG SQUARE ★★★

This charming tiny square appears in the middle of the Rue Furstenberg like a stage setting, complete with an iron lamppost and park bench. It's so perfect, it's hard to believe that the cameras aren't rolling. The Delacroix Museum, where the artist lived and worked, is at 6, Rue Furstenberg (☎ 01 44 41 86 50).

Deux Magots, facing the church, is an experience to remember. In the afternoon, the sunlit terraces are equally crowded. Prices are expensive, but worth it for the experience.

❽ Buci Market ★★
At the intersection of the Rue de Buci and the Rue de Seine. Open every day (exc. Mon.).

This is *the* Left Bank market, especially on Sundays, when the streets are packed with a very Parisian clientèle crowding around the abundance of fruits and vegetables. Even if you're not here to do your weekly shopping, it's a great place to see a real French market.

Place Saint-Sulpice and the Carrefour de l'Odéon

Just a stone's throw from the bustling Boulevard Saint-Germaine stands the Place Saint-Sulpice, with the austere Saint-Sulpice church on the east side and Visconti's superb Fountain of the Four Bishops as its centrepiece. The surrounding narrow streets are full of shops and restaurants and the Carrefour de l'Odéon, under the statue of Danton is a great meeting place for a night on the town.

❶ Saint-Sulpice Church (Église de St. Sulpice) ★★★

Place Saint-Sulpice, 75006.

Walk past the Servandoni façade and go straight to the frescoes painted by Delacroix (1849-1861). To the right of the immense nave, Jacob is still wrestling the angel, while on the opposite wall, *Heliodorus Driven from the Temple* depicts the Syrian at the base of a staircase, under a swirl of fabric.

❷ Avant-Scène ★★

4, Pl. de l'Odéon, 75006
☎ **01 46 33 12 40**
Open Tue.-Sat. 10.30am-1pm, 2.30-7pm. Closed Aug.

'Avant' as in avant-garde, 'scène' as in a stage set, this is the place for designers who share Élisabeth Delacarte's taste for Baroque and Art Deco styles, and a determination to move on from the sharp-edged style of the 1980s. You'll find Garouste and Bonetti, Van der Straeten, Dubreuil and Brazier-Jones here.

❸ Maison de Famille ★★

29, Rue Saint-Sulpice, 75006
☎ **01 40 46 97 47**
Open Mon.-Sat. 10.30am-7pm.

The two floors of this shop look as if they belong in a real home. The soft natural colours set the tone.

Every piece of furniture has a story to tell and even the smallest object seems familiar somehow. The table linen, plates,

❹ PLANTS AND FLOWERS

If you follow the Rue Saint-Sulpice to the Carrefour de l'Odéon, you'll walk past the windows of the florist, **Christian Tortu**. Just like everyone else, you'll have to stop and take a look at the lovely, sophisticated floral and plant arrangements. This is one of the best florists in Paris (see p. 13).

glasses and clothes all have a French charm. Prices for plates start from from 25F.

❺ Western House ★
23, Rue des Canettes, 75006
☎ 01 43 54 71 17
Open Mon. 1-7pm, Tue.-Sat. 10am-7.15pm.

This is where to buy yourself a cowboy outfit. You'll find jeans, boots, belts, chequered shirts and cowboy hats – all imported from America over the past 33 years.

Western House is constantly adding to its vast and exclusive stock. A touch of Arizona in the heart of Paris.

❻ Casa Bini ★★
36, Rue Grégoire-de-Tours, 75006
☎ 01 46 34 05 60
Open Sun. & Mon. 7.30-11pm, Tues.-Sat. 12.30-2.30pm, 7.30-11pm. Menu at 250-350F.

Anna Bini arrived from Florence with her bags packed with olive oil and other delicious products from Italy. Her shop was an immediate success. Parisians love the simplicity of her food with its hint of delicate Tuscan flavours.

❼ Le Café de la Mairie ★★
8, Pl. Saint-Sulpice, 75006
☎ 01 43 26 67 82
Open every day 7am-2am. Closed Sun.

It can be hard to find a seat to enjoy a coffee or delicious sandwich on this terrace, which looks onto the tower of the church. Inside the neon-lit, beige-coloured room, the locals – intellectuals, actors and students – stay late into the night.

❽ Tradition Renouée ★★
8, Rue de l'Odéon, 75006
☎ 01 40 51 08 67
Open Mon.-Sat. 11.30am-7pm.

This shop has lamps, chandeliers and pillows (from 600F). Bags, belts and hundreds of small fashion or home decorating accessories, all elegantly trimmed in a whole range of colours are also on sale. You'll find an haute-couture range at *prêt-à-porter* prices.

The Latin Quarter

The streets overflow with students, Parisians going about their daily lives and, of course, tourists. The cafés stay open late and the university bookshops are full of eager readers. Since the Sorbonne was founded in the 13th century, this part of town has been the centre of learning.

The Latin Quarter is trying to retain its history and identity, despite the fast-food restaurants that are invading the Boulevard Saint-Michel.

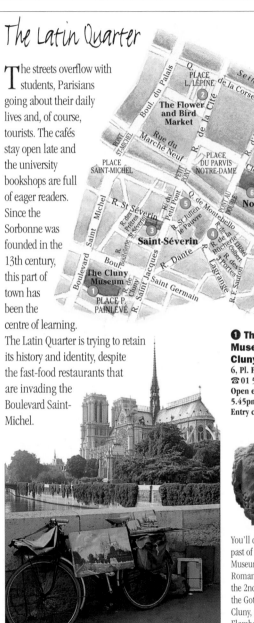

❶ The Cluny Museum (Musée de Cluny)★★★

6, Pl. Paul-Painlevé, 75005
☎ 01 53 73 78 00
Open every day 9.15am-5.45pm (exc. Tue. & hols.)
Entry charge.

You'll discover the ancient past of Paris at the Cluny Museum. From the Gallo-Roman baths, constructed in the 2nd and 3rd centuries, to the Gothic altar of the Abbots Cluny, a wonderful piece of Flamboyant architecture. The beautiful museum building alone is worth seeing. The collection is mainly medieval, including textiles, illuminated manuscripts, church furnishings and sculpture, retrieved from various churches, including Saint-Germain, Saint-Denis and Notre-Dame. The Lady with the Unicorn tapestry series is wonderful, depicting courtly love in the *millefleurs* style.

❷ THE FLOWER MARKET
Place Louis-Lépine, 75004
Open Mon.-Sat. 10am-7pm. Closed Dec.

This flower market adds a touch of colour to an otherwise rather dull built-up part of the city. It's close to Notre-Dame and on a Sunday, caged birds take the place of flowers. Enjoy a stroll through the wide range of blooms, which includes specialist varieties such as orchids. Sadly, it's one of the few remaining flower markets in the city of Paris. (See also p. 113.)

❸ Saint-Séverin Church (Église St. Séverin) ★★★
1, Rue des Prêtres-Saint-Séverin, 75005
Open Mon.-Fri. 11am-7.45pm, Sat. 11am-8pm, Sun. 9am-9pm.

This is one of the most beautiful parish churches in

Paris. It's a perfect example of Flamboyant Gothic style, and construction was completed in the early 16th century. Look at the spiralling central column and the stained glass by Jean Bazaine, the modern French painter.

❹ Shakespeare & Co ★
37, Rue de la Bûcherie, 75005
☎ 01 43 26 96 50
Open every day noon-midnight.

The shelves in this well-known shop overflow with old and new books, most of which are in English. The half-timbered façade of the building, which is situated opposite Notre-Dame and separated only by the Seine, is one of the oldest in the area. Every Sunday there's a tea party in the first floor apartment of the owner.

❺ The Tea Caddy ★
14, Rue Saint-Julien-le-Pauvre, 75005
☎ 01 43 54 15 56
Open every day (exc.Tue. & Wed.) noon-7pm.

This tearoom opened in 1928, after the invention of Hercule Poirot and Miss Marple by Agatha Christie. They would have enjoyed the English décor, the dark wooden panelling and leaded windows. Conversations are conducted in hushed tones by those enjoying the apple pies, scones and muffins in this lovely setting.

❻ Notre-Dame ★★★
Île de la Cité, 75004
Open every day 8.30am-6.45pm, (Sat. & Sun. to 7.45pm).

This cathedral is one of the finest examples of late 12th-century Gothic architecture and stands on the site of a Roman temple. Like religion itself, it has had a turbulent past – ransacked, transformed, even abandoned over the centuries. After religion was reinstated in 1804 by Napoleon, Viollet-le-Duc was commissioned to restore the buildings. Quasimodo had a magnificent view from the top, but if you want to climb up the north tower, you'll have to negotiate 387 steps.

Around the Panthéon

The area around the Pantheon at the top of the Rue de la Montagne Sainte-Geneviève has a rich and ancient past. In the Middle Ages, it was dotted first with convents and then colleges, a tradition that survives today. The architecture has a sombre, sometimes even severe, appearance, which is softened by the Luxembourg Gardens at the end of Rue Soufflot.

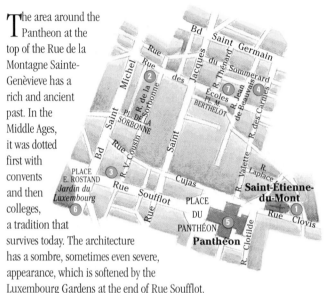

❶ Saint-Etienne-du-Mont ★★★

1, Rue Saint-Étienne-du-Mont, 75005.

This is one of the more unusual churches in Paris completed in the 17th century, with a strangely asymmetrical Renaissance-style portal and splendid rood screen. The great literary figures Racine and Pascal are buried in this elegant church, which houses the shrine of Sainte Geneviève, patron saint of Paris.

❷ Le Balzar ★★

49, Rue des Écoles, 75005
☎ 01 43 54 13 67
Open every day 8am-1am.

The waiters' outfits have remained unchanged since 1890. Dressed in black waistcoats and white aprons, they have served generations of professors, students and intellectuals. Politicians rub shoulders with journalists and people emerging from the local cinemas, and everyone enjoys the traditional French dishes in this real French brasserie.

❸ Dubois ★★

20, 24 Rue Soufflot, 75005
☎ 01 43 54 43 60
Open Tue.-Fri. 10.45am-6.30pm, Mon. & Sat. 9am-12.30pm & 1.45-6.30pm.

Artists come here to buy watercolours, oils and pastels in every conceivable colour. There are thousands of products, which can be bought by mail order from an enormous catalogue. The shop has been in this area since 1861.

❹ Mayette ★★
8, Rue des Carmes, 75005
☎ 01 43 54 13 63
Open Tue.-Sat. 10am-8pm, Mon., 2-8pm.

This shop has been in business since 1808 and is the oldest magician's shop in France. They have every kind of conjurer's trick, from the simplest to the most complex, with a whole range of books, videos and CDRoms, all stashed away in ancient drawers. It's pure magic.

❺ Panthéon ★★★
Place du Panthéon, 75005
☎ 01 44 32 18 00
Open every day 10am-6.15pm (Oct. to March), 9.30am-6.30pm (April to Sept.). Entry charge.

Louis XV made a vow to construct a church devoted to Saint Geneviève and asked the architect Soufflot to draw up the plans. Soufflot gave the church the form of a Greek cross. At the mercy of political upheavals and changing governments, the church was transformed into a pantheon, back again into a church and then finally, at Victor Hugo's death, the 'Resting Place of

Great Men'. Your footsteps will echo in the vast nave, with its 19th century frescoes by Puvis de Chavannes.

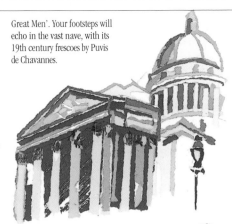

❻ LUXEMBOURG GARDENS ★★★
An idyllic spot, where Romantic poets and artists often strolled, this is a favourite haunt of Parisians. Toy sailing boats fill the octagonal pool which dominates the gardens. Take a break from the city, read your newspaper and relax just a stone's throw from the busy Boulevard Saint-Michel.

❼ Au Vieux Campeur ★★
18 shops near 48 Rue des Écoles, 75005
☎ 01 43 29 12 32
Open Mon.-Sat., 9.30am-8pm, Wed to 9pm.

If you're looking for sports equipment, this is the place to come. These shops can equip you from head to toe

for any sport, hiking, climbing, skiing, surfing (on water or snow) deep-sea diving and camping. Business has been booming since the shops opened in 1941. Mail order is also available.

Beaubourg

The square in front of the recently renovated Pompidou Centre (also simply known as the Beaubourg) is lined with fast food outlets. There's a constant stream of tourists in this area, but the artistic element still survives and even flourishes. The galleries constantly exhibit the work of well-known contemporary artists and have a very enthusiastic following. The National Museum of Modern Art (Musée National d'Art Moderne) is in the Pompidou Centre itself and has a wonderful collection.

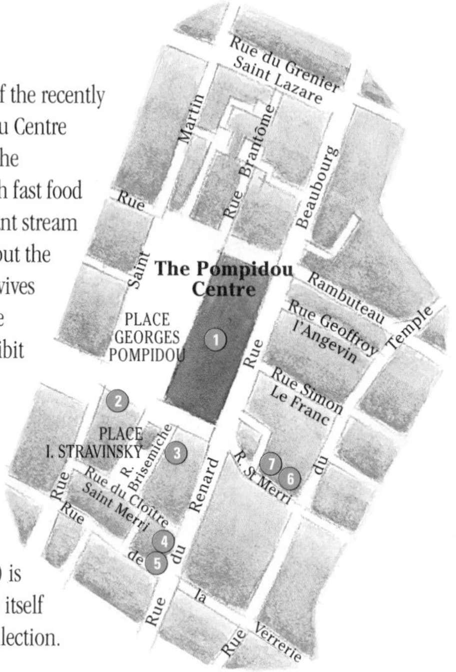

Map labels: Rue du Grenier Saint Lazare; Rue Martin; Rue Brantôme; Beaubourg; Rue Saint; The Pompidou Centre; PLACE GEORGES POMPIDOU; Rambuteau; Rue Geoffroy l'Angevin; Temple; Rue Simon Le Franc; PLACE I. STRAVINSKY; Rue du Cloître Saint Merri; R. Brisemiche; Rue Renard; R. St Merri; Rue de; Rue du; Rue de la; Rue Verrerie

❶ Le Quartier de l'Horloge

Literally the 'Clock Quarter'. The development in this area near the Beaubourg has not been a great success and there's little of great interest in the concreted courtyards and passageways. However, do go and see the unusual clock, 'The Defender of Time', by Jacques Monastier. It's a brass and steel mechanical sculpture, in which the 'defender' battles with the elements as each hour approaches. The **Perles Box** boutique nearby has a huge selection of beads, made of all kinds of materials, including glass, metal and shell, which are perfect for recreating a 60s look. Decorate your clothes with them or make bracelets

and necklaces. Kits for the latter start at 57F.

❷ The Café Beaubourg ★★
100, Rue Saint-Martin, 75004
☎ 01 48 87 63 96
Open Sun.-Thur., 8am-1am, Fri. & Sat., 8am-2am.

This stylish post-modernist café is an interesting place to stop for a coffee and watch the world go by. It was designed by Christian de Portzamparc, the architect of the Cité de la Musique La Villette, and has a timeless appeal with its post-modern colonnades.

Get away from the crowd for a while.

❸ Dame Tartine ★
2, Rue Brisemiche, 75004
☎ 01 42 77 32 22
Open every day noon-11pm.

This café attracts a very trendy crowd of artists and intellectuals. They tend to meet here in the afternoon or evening, near the Igor Stravinsky fountain by Niki de Saint-Phalle and Jean Tinguely, whose serpents and Mae West mouths hurl water into the air. Sandwiches in the café cost from 20-45F. There are some interesting paintings on the wall, as befits a café in this area.

❹ Beaubourg Gallery ★★
23, Rue du Renard, 75004
☎ 01 42 71 20 50
Open Tue.-Sat., 10.30am-1pm, 2-7pm.

You have entered the world of Marianne and Pierre Nahon. One of the first galleries to open around the Pompidou Centre, its exhibitions include both paintings and sculptures, by such artists as Arman, Ben, César, Klein

This is the place to come to see designer furniture and the latest in modern design. Pierre Staudenmeyer exhibits limited editions by Garouste and Bonetti, Olivier Gagnère and Martin Szekely. There are two floors in the gallery, and it is definitely worth a trip.

❻ Maeght Gallery ★★
12, Rue Saint-Merri, 75004
☎ 01 42 78 43 44
Open Tue.-Sat. 10am-1pm, 2-7pm.

❼ ECLACHE & CIE
10, Rue Saint-Merri, 75004 ☎ 01 42 74 62 62
Open every day noon-1am.

This very Parisian restaurant is a lovely place to relax over lunch or dinner. In the summer, you can sit at one of tables outside on the terrace alongside the building. Customers tend to be young and chic. Brunch is served from 8.30am-noon on Saturday and Sunday and costs 100F, and a meal with wine will cost 140F.

This 17th-century building offers an historical backdrop for modern works by Braque, Calder, Del Rey, Gasiorowski, Giacometti, Kuroda, Miro and Tapiès. There is also a good bookshop.

Niki de Saint-Phalle fountain on the Place Igor Stravinsky

and Andy Warhol, to name but a few.

❺ Neotu Gallery ★★
25, Rue du Renard, 75004
☎ 01 42 78 91 83
Open Mon.-Sat. 10am-7pm.

Saint-Eustache and Les Halles

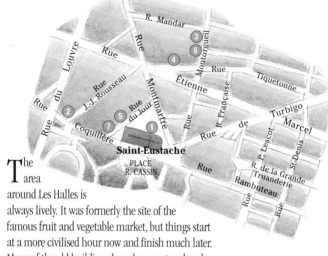

The area around Les Halles is always lively. It was formerly the site of the famous fruit and vegetable market, but things start at a more civilised hour now and finish much later. Many of the old buildings have been restored and now house trendy boutiques. It's a popular area for shoppers on Saturdays and Sunday mornings. Follow their lead and then relax over a drink in one of the many cafés. You'll see all walks of Parisian life.

❶ Saint-Eustache Church (Église St. Eustache) ★★★
2,4, Impasse Saint-Eustache, 75001.

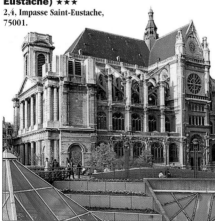

A beautiful Gothic and Renaissance church, it took over 100 years to complete. Its colourful history includes the baptism of Cardinal Richelieu, Louis XIV's first communion and the burials of Colbert, Rameau and Moliere. Berlioz gave the inaugural performance of his *Te Deum* in the church and Liszt, the first performance of his *Messe de Gran*. Its wonderful organ can be heard in concert twice every day and each day the concert schedule is attached to the door of the church.

❷ Dehillerin ★
18, Rue Coquilliere, 75001
☎ 01 42 36 53 13
Open Mon. 8am-12.30pm &
2-6pm, Tue.-Sat. 8am-6pm
(Aug. 10am-6pm).

Try to get to this shop early to avoid the crowds. On the ground floor and in the basement, you'll find every

conceivable piece of kitchen equipment. There are pots and pans of every size in copper, cast-iron or aluminium. It's a cook's dream, whether professional, amateur or just armchair.

❸ Le Centre Ville ★★
57, Rue Montorgueil, 75002
☎ 01 42 33 20 40
Open Tue.-Fri. 8am-8pm, Sat.-Sun. 9am-1pm.

This is a very Parisian bistrot with beige, slightly smoke-stained walls and a mahogany counter. It will remind you of old films from the 50s. There are only a few tables, mostly occupied by locals and a trendy set. It's not a place for an intimate chat – you'll be eating elbow to elbow with your fellow customers.

❹ Kiliwatch ★
6, Rue Tiquetonne, 75002
☎ 01 42 21 17 37
Open Tue.-Sat. 10.30am-9pm, Sun.-Mon. 1-7pm.

This is a great place for secondhand clothes in all shapes, sizes, styles and shades. You could emerge

with a whole new wardrobe, including sequinned tops, New Age or kitschy accessories and shiny bags. Rummage to your heart's content.

❺ La Droguerie ★
9, Rue du Jour, 75001
☎ 01 45 08 93 27
Open Tue.-Sat. 10.30am-6.45pm (Aug. 10.30am-1pm).

Vivid colour is just everywhere in this shop. Wool, linen,

cotton and mohair in every possible hue cover the walls. There are ribbons, beads, feathers, buttons (antique and new from 50 centimes to 150F), braids and sequins.

❻ Stohrer ★
51, Rue Montorgueil, 75002
☎ 01 42 33 38 20
Open every day 7.30am-8.30pm.

❼ AGNÈS B. ★★
2, 3, 6, 10, Rue du Jour, 75001
☎ 01 45 08 56 56
Mon.-Sat. 10am-7.30pm.

There are several branches of Agnès B., selling children's, women's and men's clothes. Her clothes have a timeless elegance and her classic jeans, shirts and dresses are mostly in white, black or natural colours. At 44, Rue Quincampoix, 75004, there's an art gallery, which is open Tue.-Sat., 10am-7pm, where Agnès B. gives designers a chance to exhibit their paintings, sculpture or photography.
☎ 01 44 54 55 90

Stohrer arrived in France along with the luggage belonging to Marie Leczinska, Louis XV's fiancée. Several years later he moved to the Rue Montorgueil and began to make his wonderful pastry creations, in particular his *Ali-Baba* and his *puits d'amour*. The shop opened in 1730 and still sells its delicious cakes. It's worth a trip just to see the sugary interior by Paul Baudry.

Around Saint-Paul

The Île Saint-Louis is the second of the two islands is in the middle of the Seine. It's a little self-contained village in the heart of the city, with tree-lined quays, classical façades and wonderful

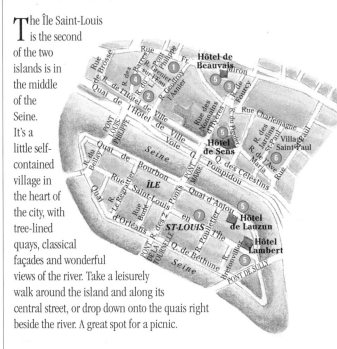

views of the river. Take a leisurely walk around the island and along its central street, or drop down onto the quais right beside the river. A great spot for a picnic.

❶ Izrael ★★
30, Rue Francois-Miron, 75004
☎ 01 42 72 66 23
Open Tue.-Sat., 9.30am-1pm & 2.30pm-7pm. Closed August.

Close your eyes and you'll think you are in a Middle Eastern spice shop, with all its exotic scents. Open your eyes and you'll be overwhelmed by a chaos of colour, with sacks, crates and boxes of ingredients piled high, with

every spice you could possibly want. It's a cook's dream.

❷ Calligrane ★★
4, 6, Rue du Pont-Louis-Philippe, 75004
☎ 01 40 27 00 74
Open Tue.-Sat., 11am-7pm.

Every kind of paper is for sale here, some even inlaid with exotic wood. Choose from parchment (great for lampshades), Japanese folded paper and pens and pencils of all kinds and colours.

❸ Galerie Sâling ★★
14, Rue de Fourcy, 75004
☎ 01 40 27 95 75
Open Mon.-Sat. 10.30am-
8pm, Sun. 2-7pm.

Most of the jewellery, clothes and carpets in this gallery come from Afghanistan. It specialises in Central Asian crafts and has magnificent silver rings set with semi-precious stones. Some of the spice boxes from Pakistan are particularly beautiful. Jewellery is available for every budget, from 100F to 100,000F.

❹ Papier + ★★
9, Rue du Pont-Louis-
Philippe, 75004
☎ 01 42 77 70 49
Open Mon.-Sat. noon-7pm.

This shop was amongst the first to treat paper as an art form, and it sells notebooks and journals in every conceivable hue, recycled paper by the kilo and 70 different coloured pencils.

❺ Private Mansions (Hôtels) ★★★
Enjoy a tour of some of the *hôtels*, or town houses in this area, with their wonderful history and architecture. Queen Margot once lived in the Hôtel de Sens at 1, Rue du Figuier, with its medieval towers. The Hôtel de Beauvais on the Rue Francois-Miron was home for Mozart in 1763, and Chopin and Delacroix dined at the most famous house on the island, the Hôtel Lambert, on Rue Saint-Louis-en-l'Île. The Hôtel de Lauzun with its beautiful gilded balcony and Classical façade hosted dinners at which Baudelaire was present.

❻ Saint-Paul Village ★★
23, 25, Rue Saint-Paul, 75004
Open Thur.-Mon. 11am-
7pm. Closed Tue. & Wed.

An antiques market which is held on the street and in a courtyard, in a car-free zone.

ARISTOTE
☎ 01 42 77 92 94 Trinkets and small items of furniture.
LE PUCERON CHINEUR
☎ 01 42 72 88 20 Silverware.
LA SOURIS VERTE
☎ 01 42 74 79 76 Linen, lace, glassware and trinkets.
AU DÉBOTTÉ
☎ 01 48 04 85 20 18th century furniture, paintings, gilded and sculpted wood.

❼ L'ÎLE SAINT-LOUIS ★★★
At the end of the 17th century, the island was considered an extension of the Marais quarter, having been transformed from swampy pastureland to an elegant residential area. It has retained its village atmosphere, and you can spend many a happy hour, strolling in its quiet streets at any time of day, even in poor weather. It's an intimate and romantic quarter, with great views of the river. At night you can watch the illuminated *bateaux-mouches* (pleasure boats) sail past.

PASSE-PARTOUT
☎ 01 42 72 94 94 Locks and keys, corkscrews, nutcrackers, old knives, everything for writers and smokers.

The Marais

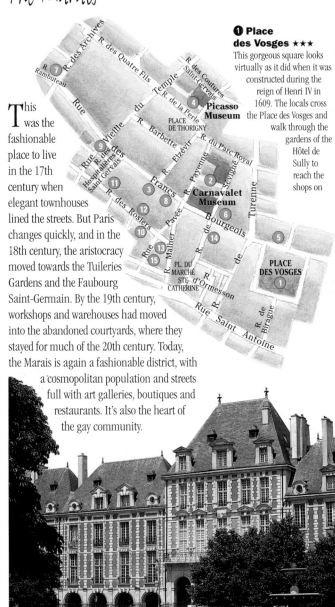

❶ Place des Vosges ★★★

This gorgeous square looks virtually as it did when it was constructed during the reign of Henri IV in 1609. The locals cross the Place des Vosges and walk through the gardens of the Hôtel de Sully to reach the shops on

This was the fashionable place to live in the 17th century when elegant townhouses lined the streets. But Paris changes quickly, and in the 18th century, the aristocracy moved towards the Tuileries Gardens and the Faubourg Saint-Germain. By the 19th century, workshops and warehouses had moved into the abandoned courtyards, where they stayed for much of the 20th century. Today, the Marais is again a fashionable district, with a cosmopolitan population and streets full with art galleries, boutiques and restaurants. It's also the heart of the gay community.

the Rue Saint-Antoine. Stroll around the arcade and do a spot of window-shopping at the antique stores, bookshops, art galleries and boutiques. At night, you may feel the shadow of Victor Hugo, who lived here for many years, accompanying you on one of the best walks in Paris.

❷ Carnavalet Museum (Musée Carnavalet) ★★★
23, Rue de Sévigné, 75003
☎ 01 42 72 21 13
Open every day (exc. Mon.) 10am.-5.45pm. Entry charge.

One of the few Renaissance mansions in Paris. The museum traces the history of Paris until the present day

with emphasis on the Revolution. There are paintings by Hubert Robert

covering the latter and memorabilia of the royal family. End your tour with the Art Nouveau decor designed by Mucha for the Fouquet Jewellery Boutique. There's also a great bookshop and museum shop.

❸ Paris-Musées ★
29, a, Rue des Francs-Bourgeois, 75004
☎ 01 42 74 13 02
Open Tue.- Sat. 11am-7pm, Mon. 2-7pm, Sun. 11am-6.30pm.

With simple materials – cardboard and painted wood – and enormous talent, Jean Oddes decorated this shop in the 17th-century style. This is where you'll find tableware and household items copied from works in the collections of the City of Paris museum.

❹ Picasso Museum (Musée Picasso) ★★★
Hôtel Salé, 5, Rue de Thorigny, 75004
☎ 01 42 71 25 21
Open every day (exc. Tue.) 9.30am-5.50pm. Entry charge.

This museum has a large collection covering the whole extent of Picasso's work, housed in one of the most beautiful *hôtels* in the Marais. It's a must, if only to see the *Self-Portrait* from his blue period, the *Still Life with Cane Chair* from his Cubist years and *Pan's Flute* from his classical period. Of Picasso's sculptures don't miss the amazing *Guenon and Child*.

Also see the most beautiful Matisse painting in Paris, *Still Life with Oranges*. The bookshop has a large selection of art books.

❺ Les Deux Orphelines ★★
21, Pl. des Vosges, 75003
☎ 01 42 72 63 97
Open Mon.-Fri. 11am-7pm. Closed Aug.

As you walk through the door, you'll enter into a world of charming country-style antiques. Choose from a turn of the century straw armchair, a pale wooden pedestal table, a landscape in watercolour or a framed bouquet of flowers.

❻ Autour du Monde Home ★

8, Rue des Francs-Bourgeois, 75003
☎ 01 42 77 06 08

Open Tue.-Sat. 10.30am-7.30pm, Sun. from 1pm, Mon. from 11.30am.

This shop concentrates on the natural look, with lots of recycled furniture (in American barnwood), and traditional antiques from the United States and Portugal. There are clothes as well, with the 'basics' collections by Bensimon, in linen and cotton, of course.

❼ Les Mille Feuilles ★★

2, Rue Rambuteau, 75003
☎ 01 42 78 32 93
Open Tue.-Fri. 10am-12.30pm, 1.30-8pm, Sat. to 7pm.

Located on the corner of the Rue des Archives, this enchanting shop draws people from every corner of Paris. Vases and baskets of flowers are scattered on pedestal

tables, garden tables and secondhand chairs. Everything in this chaotic, but delightful shop is for sale.

❽ Jean-Pierre de Castro ★★

17, Rue des Francs-Bourgeois, 75004
☎ 01 42 72 04 00
Open Tues.-Sat. 10.30am-7pm, Sun. 11am-1pm, 2-7pm, Mon. 2-7pm.

All kinds of silver objects are stacked floor to ceiling here. There are pieces from the 17th century through to the 1950s, and almost all (90%) are secondhand. There are tea and coffee services, plates and serving dishes as far as the eye can see. Silver-plated forks and spoons are sold by weight. Now's the time to overhaul your table settings.

SUNDAY SHOPPING

The Marais is one of the few areas in Paris where most of the shops stay open on Sunday. It's good to know if you still have last minute shopping to do. It's a good idea to check the opening times, because the hours often differ from weekdays. But be forewarned – you won't be alone!

❾ L'Art du Bureau ★

47, Rue des Francs-Bourgeois, 75004
☎ 01 48 87 57 97
Open Mon.- Sat. 10.30am-1.30pm & 2.30-7pm, Sun. 2-7pm.

This shop stands out on a street consisting mainly of clothes shops. You can buy everything you need for the office, in wood, pewter or metal. There are diaries, files and pens, including famous names such as Mont-Blanc and Omas.

10 L'Éclaireur ★★
3B, Rue des Rosiers, 75004
☎ 01 48 87 10 22
Open Tue.-Sat. 11am-7pm, Mon. 2-7pm.

A former printing works, the owners have adapted this shop with great care and taste. There are two floors, with clothes draped over designer furniture. The style is rather avant-garde with most of the jewellery and glass pieces by well-known designers. The creations of the Italian designer Fornasetti are sold exclusively in this emporium.

11 Chez Marianne ★
2, Rue des Hospitaliers-Saint-Gervais, 75004
☎ 01 42 72 18 86
Open every day 12.30pm-midnight.

Marianne is on the corner of the street, right in the heart of an area of craftsmen's shops and *prêt-à-porter* boutiques. The walls are decorated with bottles, and near the door there is a delicatessen counter with drawers full of different dried fruits and spices. Notice the paintings over the bar and the Eastern European specialities.

12 Hariet de Prague ★★
6, Rue des Rosiers, 75004
☎ 01 42 77 15 87
Open Tue.-Sat., 11am-7pm.

This is just like a milliner's shop, where you can find the perfect little straw hat covered with flowers or feathers, and a selection of styles that range from extravagant to classical. There are lovely wedding gowns plus evening and cocktail dresses.

13 Le Loir dans la Théière ★★
3, Rue des Rosiers, 75004
☎ 01 42 72 90 61
Open Mon.-Fri. 11.30am-6pm, Sat. & Sun.10.30am-6pm.

Lewis Carroll would have loved the English atmosphere of this tearoom, where you can spend hours reading magazines and newspapers in comfortable old armchairs, around ancient tables. Enjoy the art exhibitions and delicious pastries.

14 Losco ★
20, Rue de Sévigné, 75004
☎ 01 48 04 39 93
Open Tue.-Sat. 11am-7pm, Mon. 2-7pm, Sun. 3-7pm.

This is a belt shop *par excellence*. The decor is in wood, and the smell of leather pervades the atmosphere. Losco is a craftsman who will make a belt to fit you as you watch. Choose your own colour and buckle.

15 Caravane ★★★
6, Rue Pavée, 75004
☎ 01 44 61 04 20
Open Tue.-Sat. 11am-7pm.

A real Aladdin's cave. Embroidered wall hangings from Central Asia, cotton and appliquéd fabrics from India, carpets from Morocco, at very reasonable prices, Ashanti and Lunda weavings from Africa and Foutas from Tunisia, are all here.

Bastille and the Faubourg Saint-Antoine

There are still a few remaining workshops and craftsmen still keep alive the tradition of furniture-making, in the alleys and courtyards of this historic district. In the evenings, the bars and restaurants attract a mixture of city and suburban folk. On a Friday night the bikers converge on the Place de la Bastille in front of the Opera to give their unique, but noisy performance.

Marsautet chairs an open discussion with a lively and very diverse group. It's advisable to arrive around 10am, as it's a very popular event. On Friday nights you can enjoy a game of chess or backgammon, or listen to jazz. There are also art and photography exhibitions.

❶ Café des Phares ★★

7, pl. de la Bastille, 75004
☎ 01 42 72 04 70
Open every day
7.15am-3am.

They serve Italian-style sandwiches and great coffee here. At 11am every Sunday, the philosopher Marc

❷ Bofinger ★★

5, Rue de la Bastille, 75004
☎ 01 42 72 87 82
Open every day noon-1am. Fixed price menu for 119F and 169F (lunch).

When this brasserie first opened in 1864 it served food 24 hours a day. This is no longer the case, but the mission of the original owner, M. Bofinger, continues to this

day to provide delicious food in a congenial atmosphere. It was the first place to serve draught beer and has excellent shellfish and grilled meats. It's a little calmer on the first floor where you can admire the frescoes by the Alsatian artist Hansi.

❸ Jean-Paul Gaultier Gallery ★★

30, Faubourg Saint-Antoine, 75012
☎ 01 44 68 84 84
Open Mon. 11.30am-7.30pm, Tue.-Sat. 10.30am-7.30pm.

In this store you will find Gaultier's three clothing collections, plus furniture, perfume and other items. The floor is decorated with mosaic zodiac signs and from the ceiling stars hang in a rainbow of colours. On the walls are *métro* tiles and trick mirrors. The designer himself created the interior. There's also a store at 6, Rue Vivienne, 75002.

❹ Bastille Opera (Opéra Bastille) ★★

Place de la Bastille, 75011
☎ 01 44 73 13 99

Box office open every day 9am-7pm, ☎ 08 36 69 78 68

This is one of the most controversial opera houses in Europe, a legacy of the Mitterand era and an immense, curved glass building, whose modern design, by Carlos Ott, shocked many. It was considered to be too far from the centre, the quality of its acoustics was questioned and the early years were fraught with power struggles, rivalries and financial difficulties. The

auditorium seats 2,700 people, most of whom nowadays are more interested in the quality of the singers' voices, the orchestra and the imaginative power of the sets.

❺ Café du Passage ★★

12, Rue de Charonne, 75012
☎ 01 49 29 97 64
Open every day 6pm-2am, Sat. 2pm-2am.

This late night bar is very British in style. Architects, film producers and local artists mingle in the comfortable lounge with its deep red armchairs. It's an unusual and interesting wine bar, quite unexpected in this area.

❻ L'Arbre à Lettres ★★

62, Faubourg Saint-Antoine, 75012
☎ 01 53 33 83 23
Open Mon.-Sat. 10am-8pm, Sun., 2.30-7pm. Closed Sundays in summer.

❼ RUE DE LAPPE

This street has quite a reputation. Young Parisian couples would dance the night away in one of the many clubs. Balajo (at no. 9) still continues the tradition and is a good place to dance *le rock*. With the arrival of Japanese and Tex-Mex restaurants, the street has lost some of its former appeal.

This bookshop is sandwiched between two furniture stores and has a slightly sober interior, except for the room containing art books. It opens onto the Bel-Air courtyard, which is one of the most beautiful in the area. Not much has changed since the 19th century.

Rooms and restaurants

There are more than a thousand places to stay in Paris, mostly two- and three-star hotels. Choose one in your price range, of course (bearing in mind that Paris is an expensive city, hotels included). Paris is renowned for its cuisine of course, though it is possible to eat badly here, so select your restaurant with care.

HOTELS

If you want to join the international crowd choose the Opéra, the Madeleine or the grand boulevards. The Champs-Elysées area is chic and expensive, the 7th, 9th and 16th *arrondissements* are quiet and residential, and the Left Bank is younger, livelier and often better value.

A double room costs from about 180-350F in a one-star, 350-500F in a two-star, and 500-900F in a three-star hotel. For four-star hotels of course, prices can go much higher. The star ratings are established by the Ministry of Tourism and the Paris Prefecture according to various criteria such as the size of the rooms (12 m²/ 39sq ft minimum in a three-star hotel), the level of comfort, and whether or not there are night porters and bilingual or trilingual staff. Be aware that the standard will vary from one district to another and from one hotel to the next.

BOOKING A ROOM

From April to November, you should book your room by phone, confirm by fax or mail, and then send a cheque for the deposit (10-15% of the price), or give your credit card number. The room will be held for you till 6pm on the day you are due to arrive, or later if you give advance warning. Otherwise the hotel can keep your deposit as compensation for your non-arrival. Excluding the months of May, June, September and October, you can try to negotiate the price of a luxury room or get a reduction of 30-40%. Success is not guaranteed, but why not try anyway. A word of warning for visitors from the US, rooms will be much smaller than those you are used to at home.

If you visit Paris out of season, but during a major event like the Motor Show or the Agricultural Show, you should also book ahead. The Paris Tourist Office can help you find and book accommodation (see p. 31). There is also a centralised hotel reservation service, call: ☎ 01 43 59 12 12

EXTRAS

If you have children, you can ask for an extra bed in a double room or negotiate a suite. The price of a room does not always include breakfast. Expect to pay from 30-80F depending on the hotel. A TV in your room is a plus, but watch out for those minibars if you have one. The price of the small bottles adds up quickly and your bill may come as a big surprise.

TOURIST ACCOMMODATION, BED AND BREAKFASTS

You can also find tourist accomodation in private houses. Try *Tourisme chez l'habitant*, 15, Rue des Pas-Perdus, 95804, Cergy-St-Christophe (BP 8338) ☎ 01 34 25 44 44 (a double room with private bathroom will cost around 168-206F, breakfast included; you will also have to pay a 50F registration fee). Inexpensive accommodation for students and anyone else on a tight budget: Résidence Bastille, 151, Ave Ledru-Rollin, 75004, ☎ 01 42 72 72 09; or UCRIF, 27, Rue de Turbigo, 75002, ☎ 01 40 26 57 64. The Centre International

LATE-NIGHT DINING

Most places stop serving sometime around 10 or 11pm. If you want something to eat later than that, you can try one of the following restaurants, which stay open all night: *La Maison d'Alsace*, 39, Champs-Élysées, 75008, ☎ 01 53 93 97 00; *Pied de Cochon*, 6, Rue Coquillière, 75001, ☎ 01 40 13 77 00; *Grand Café*, 4, Blvd des Capucines, 75009, ☎ 01 43 12 19 00. You can also choose from one of the following chains: the *Hippopotamus*, *Le Bistro Romain* and *Léon*, for example, all stay open late, as do many fast-food restaurants. Just don't expect a gourmet's paradise.

de Séjour de Paris, 17, Blvd Kellermann, 75013, ☎ 01 44 16 37 38, is like a two-star youth hostel, where a double room with breakfast costs 156F per person, and a dormitory room for eight, 113F per person, breakfast included.

You can also sleep in a tent or park a mobile home in the Bois de Boulogne, at the Allée du bord de l'eau (quite an experience)! ☎ 01 45 24 30 00, open all year round.

RESTAURANTS

Paris caters for every price range and all kinds of tastes, including typically French or exotic cuisine, gourmet

dishes or regional specialities. You'll find small bistros, lively brasseries and sophisticated restaurants. If the place is well-known, it's wise to call ahead to book your table.

Unfortunately, tourist areas are not always the best places to eat, and you may end up paying more than the meal is actually worth. This applies particularly in Montmartre, Montparnasse and Les Halles (with a few notable exceptions, of course).

THE BILL, PLEASE

Menu prices always indicate the price per person. *Prix fixe* offers a menu with a rather limited choice at a set price, which may or may not include drinks (certain menus offer a main course plus a glass of wine). The average price of a good meal in Paris is higher than elsewhere in France. It's possible to have a meal for 70F in a basic restaurant, but the price for dinner generally starts from 100-120F per person.

A 15% service charge is already included in the price, but it is customary to tip the waiter or waitress, especially if the food or service was exceptional (up to 10F in a bistrot, more in a nice restaurant). Most restaurants sell cigarettes if you're desperate to smoke. In top-notch establishments, you can even order your favourite Havana cigar, provided, of course, that your table is in the area reserved for smokers.

CAFÉS, BARS AND ICE-CREAM SHOPS

Taverne Henri-IV

13, Pl. du Pont-Neuf, 75001
☎ 01 43 54 27 90
Metro Pont-Neuf
Open Mon.-Fri. noon-8.30pm,
Sat. noon-4pm. Closed Sun.
and at weekends in summer.

Between La Samaritaine and the
Latin Quarter, this is an excellent
place for a glass of wine – a
Beaujolais, Chinon or Morgon
– with toasted sandwiches and
charcuterie from the Aveyron, or
a selection of typical French
cheeses (from around 80F).

Berthillon

31, Rue Saint-Louis-en-
l'Île, 75004
☎ 01 43 54 31 61
Metro Pont Marie

Open every day 10am-8pm
Closed Mon. & Tue. out of
season.

In summer, you'll have to queue
(especially on a Sunday), but it's
worth it for the melt-in-the-mouth
ice creams and sorbets. Try melon,
mandarin, raspberry or pear.

Le Flore en l'Île

42, Quai d'Orléans, 75004
☎ 01 43 29 88 27
Metro Pont Marie
Open every day 8.30am-2am.

This is the best place to go
if you get a sudden midnight
craving for a cup of tea with

chocolate cake or crème brûlée.
It's ideally located on the Île
Saint-Louis.

Café Maure de la Mosquée

38, Rue Geoffroy-Saint-
Hilaire, 75005
☎ 01 43 31 18 14
Metro Jussieu
Open every day 8.30am-
midnight.

It's crowded at weekends, but

you're guaranteed an exotic
experience. Sip a glass of mint tea
and soak up the atmosphere. The
place is decorated with Moroccan
mosaics and gazelle horns. Great
value and you can relax in the
hammam afterwards.

Harry's Bar

5, Rue Daunou, 75002
☎ 01 42 61 71 14
Metro Opéra
Open every day 10.30am-4am.

This is an institution dating
from 1911, a favourite of
Hemingway and Fitzgerald.
Enjoy pure malt whisky, or an
exotic cocktail with a lively crowd.

Damman's

20, Rue du Cardinal-
Lemoine, 75005
☎ 01 46 33 61 30
Metro Cardinal-Lemoine
Open Mon.-Sat. 2-6pm
(8pm in summer). Closed
weekends and hols.

Depending upon your mood and
your appetite, nibble on a tasty
little salad or gorge yourself on
a huge variety of ices.

La Pagode

57 Rue de Babylone, 75007
☎ 01 45 56 10 67
Metro St-François-Xavier.
Open Mon.-Sat. 4-10pm,
Sun. 2-8pm.

This avant-garde cinema with its rich red Chinese decor, is a good place for a slice of apple tart and a cup of tea outside in the garden. It's especially pleasant when the weather is fine and will cost around 40F.

Café Blanc

40, Rue François-1er, 75008,
☎ 01 53 67 30 13

Metro George-V
Open Mon.-Fri. 8am-7pm,
Sat. from 11am. Closed Sun.

If you can't afford a chic little designer dress, console yourself with a savoury tart or a very reasonably priced 'dish of the day'.

La Coupole

102, Blvd. Montparnasse, 75006
☎ 01 43 20 14 20
Metro Vavin
Open every day 7.30am-2am.

You can have a drink on the terrace, enjoy seafood or steak tartare, or take part in an afternoon dance. This famous 1930s *brasserie* with its painted pillars and ceiling, is still worth a visit, even if it has lost some of its original charm.

L'Écluse

64, Rue François-1er, 75008,
☎ 01 47 20 77 09
Metro George-V
Open every day 11.30am-1am.

This wine bar is an institution, if a bit pricey. Stop by for a glass (or bottle) of Bordeaux, Chateau La Lagune, Saint-Estèphe, Pauillac or Saint-Émilion, and enjoy a cheese platter with your drink.

HOTELS

The prices given here are for double rooms, with or without breakfast, and are a guide only. Most rooms have cable television, a minibar and a safe. Hotel staff will usually speak some English.

Tuileries ★★★

10, Rue Hyacinthe, 75001
☎ 01 42 61 04 17
01 49 27 91 56
Metro Tuileries 790-1200F.

This is a rare haven of peace behind the Place Vendôme. The restored 18th-century listed building was once the home of Marie Antoinette's lady-in-waiting. It has 26 air-conditioned rooms, each with a bathroom, TV, safe, antique furniture and paintings. The service is exceptional, and the guests are mostly regulars.

Britannique ★★★

20, Ave. Victoria, 75001
☎ 01 42 33 74 59
01 42 33 82 65
Metro Châtelet
830-950F, breakfast: 58F.

Forty very comfortable rooms await you here, in a quiet avenue just a stone's throw from the bookstalls along the Seine. This hotel was opened in 1840 by English owners and it still has a British atmosphere with its leather armchairs and Turner reproductions. You'll find that 60% of the guests are American or British). Internet access is also available.

Saintonge ★★★

16, Rue de Saintonge, 75003
☎ 01 42 77 91 13
01 48 87 76 41
Metro Rambuteau or Filles-du-Calvaire
490-560F, breakfast: 45F.

This hotel, behind the national archives in the heart of the Marais, has picturesque stone walls, exposed beams and a vaulted breakfast room. The facilities are very modern and the atmosphere friendly and pleasant.

Pavillon de la Reine ★★★★

28, Pl. des Vosges, 75003
☎ 01 40 29 19 19
01 40 29 19 20

Metro Saint-Paul or Bastille
1850-2100F.

Step back in time in this idyllic, peaceful hotel, situated in one of the most delightful Parisian squares. It has 55 rooms each overlooking a courtyard or small garden. Total comfort with *Grand Siècle* refinement and Louis XIII furniture awaits in this fabulously luxurious hotel.

Caron de Beaumarchais ★★★

12, Rue Vieille-du-Temple, 75003 ☎ 01 42 72 34 12
01 42 72 34 63
Metro Hôtel de Ville or St-Paul
690-770F, breakfast: 54F.

The playwright Beaumarchais used to live near here, and his *Mariage de Figaro* inspired the decor of the 19 charming air-conditioned rooms, with their period fabric designs, antique furniture and hand-crafted, painted bathroom tiles. There is also a Louis XVI fireplace in the lounge.

Les Deux Îles ★★★

59, Rue Saint-Louis-en-l'Île, 75004
☎ 01 43 26 13 35
01 46 34 60 25
Metro Pont-Marie
840F, breakfast: 50F.

This hotel on the Île Saint-Louis has a charm all of its own. It has 17 small rooms, all well insulated with blue-and-white Portuguese-style tiled bathrooms and Provençal fabrics.

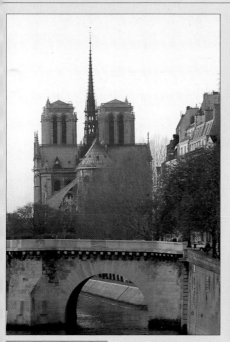

floors. There is a small garden too. All in all, a delightful place to stay in the Latin Quarter.

L'Abbaye★★★

10, Rue Cassette, 75006,
☎ 01 45 44 38 11
🅵 01 45 48 07 86
Metro Saint-Sulpice
960-1900F inc. breakfast

You'll be warmly welcomed in this former convent, now a charming and quiet hotel. It has 42 rooms (not very large but all different and comfortable), a courtyard and garden (pleasant for breakfast in the summer). An attractive combination of tradition and contemporary design.

Saint-Dominique ★★

62, Rue Saint-Dominique, 75007
☎ 01 47 05 51 44
🅵 01 47 05 81 28
Metro Invalides
520-620F, breakfast: 40F.

Notre-Dame ★★★

19, Rue Maître-Albert, 75005
☎ 01 43 26 79 00
🅵 01 46 33 50 11
Metro St-Michel or Maubert-Mutualité
690-750F, breakfast: 40F.

This hotel has 34 rooms with antique furniture (some with exposed beams), bathroom, safe and TV and is in a quiet spot just opposite the cathedral. There is also a magnificent Aubusson tapestry in the lounge. The service is faultless.

Select ★★★

1, Pl. de la Sorbonne, 75005
☎ 01 46 34 14 80
🅵 01 46 34 51 79
Metro Luxembourg
650-805F, buffet-breakfast: 40F.

This hotel has an original, contemporary decor with exposed beams and a central indoor patio, with a glass dome covered in plants. There are 67 spacious, air-conditioned rooms, a basement bar and a waterfall. The hotel is near the Luxembourg Gardens, perfect for a Sunday morning jog.

Le Clos Médicis ★★★

56, Rue Monsieur-le-Prince, 75006
☎ 01 43 29 10 80
🅵 01 43 54 26 90
Metro Luxembourg
790-990F, breakfast: 60F

This was a private residence in the late 19th century. Today it is a hotel with 37 air-conditioned and well insulated rooms and suites. There are touches of Provence in the stone, wood and wrought-iron, with yellow-ochre colours, bright fabrics, antique furniture and tiled bathroom

This hotel is in a restored 18th century building (notice the original beams in the reception area) with a summer patio. The 34 rooms have pine furniture. There's a village atmosphere in this quarter. Spend the morning at the Musée d'Orsay then go shopping in the Opera district and walk to the Champs-Élysées.

Bersoly's

28, Rue de Lille, 75007
☎ 01 42 60 73 79
G 01 49 27 05 55
Metro Rue du Bac
660-760F, breakfast: 50F.

This hotel, situated in the antique-dealers' area near the Musée d'Orsay, was a convent in the 17th century. The 16 air-conditioned rooms are named after painters (Picasso, Renoir, Lautrec, Gauguin) and are decorated with reproductions of their works. A stone staircase leads down to the vaulted breakfast rooms.

Franklin Roosevelt ★★★

18, Rue Clément-Marot, 75008
☎ 01 53 57 49 50
G 01 47 20 44 30
Metro Franklin Roosevelt
945-1500F, breakfast: 65F.

In one of the most luxurious areas of the capital, the Franklin Roosevelt is like a private mansion with its comfortable lounges and wooden panelling. The 45 rooms (with bathroom) are decorated with trompe-l'oeil paintings, or Japanese-style cool relaxing colours.

Hôtel Beau Manoir

6, rue de l'Arcade 75008 Paris - Tél : (1) 42 66 03 07

Beau Manoir ★★★★

6, Rue de l'Arcade, 75008
☎ 01 42 66 03 07
G 01 42 68 03 00
Metro Madeleine
1200F inc. buffet breakfast.

This charming hotel near the Faubourg Saint-Honoré and the department stores has 29 spacious rooms and three suites, with

furniture from the Drouot auction rooms. There is a magnificent Aubusson tapestry in the lounge, and a calm and comfortable atmosphere. The buffet-breakfast is served in vaulted cellars. For about 150F, you can enjoy a meal in your room, prepared by apprentice chefs from the Trois Gros restaurant.

Lido ★★★

4, Passage de la Madeleine, 75008
☎ 01 42 66 27 37
G 01 42 66 61 23
Metro Madeleine or Auber
980-1100F inc. breakfast.

This calm, friendly hotel is quite a find, located so near the noisy streets around the shopping districts. It has 32 air-conditioned rooms (all with bathrooms), decorated in bright colours. You can eat in your room if you wish but a buffet-breakfast is also served in a vaulted cellar.

Galileo ★★★

54, Rue Galilée, 75008
☎ 01 47 20 66 06
𝔽 01 47 20 67 17

Metro George-V
950F, breakfast: 50F.

This is an exclusive hotel in an exclusive area. There are 27 air-conditioned rooms, with designer furniture and bathrooms in light-grey marble. There is a fireplace and a wintergarden, as well as a real garden. Your stay will be very comfortable.

Tronchet ★★★

22, rue Tronchet, 75008
☎ 01 47 42 26 14
𝔽 01 49 24 03 82
Metro Madeleine
580-860F, breakfast: 50F.

In the heart of Paris, this hotel is just a stone's throw from the department stores, the Opera district, the theatres, and the bistrots in the Rue Daunou. There is also a public car park nearby, a rarity in Paris. The 34 renovated rooms are all tastefully decorated, and most are air-conditioned. Breakfast is served in the vaulted dining-room, unless, of course, you prefer to have breakfast in bed.

Union Hôtel ★★★

44, Rue Hamelin, 75016
☎ 01 45 53 14 95
𝔽 01 47 55 94 79
Metro Iéna
750-870F, continental
breakfast: 45F.

Near the Place Charles de Gaulle *Étoile*, this charming, quiet hotel with 41 rooms has recently been renovated. All the rooms have a television, minibar and marble bathroom. There's a small indoor garden where you can enjoy breakfast in fine weather. The service is always good.

Pergolèse ★★★★

3, Rue Pergolèse, 75116
☎ 01 53 64 04 04
𝔽 01 53 64 04 40
Metro Argentine
1250-1700F, breakfast: 70-95F.

The interior designer and architect Rena Dumas has left his mark here. The interior is sophisticated, but daring, with a curved glass wall, bright-blue

pillars on sienna walls and light-coloured ash furniture. Dumas paid careful attention to detail in each of the 40 air-conditioned rooms, which all have a writing desk, mini-bar and television. It's beautifully simple and elegant.

RESTAURANTS

Muscade

66, Galerie Montpensier, 75001
☎ 01 42 97 51 36
Metro Palais-Royal
Open every day 12.15pm-midnight
A la carte 148-188F.

Cocteau's apartment, just above this restaurant, was the inspiration for the black-and-white marble decor. Enjoy gambas, squid and salmon. There's a tearoom serving delicious chocolate and orange tarts, and a terrace for those sunny afternoons.

Le Grand Colbert

2-4, Rue Vivienne, 75002
☎ 01 42 86 87 88
Metro Richelieu-Drouot
Open every day noon-1am
Evening valet parking
Menu 155F.

You'll find a fixed-price menu at 155F with a choice of three starters, three main courses, three desserts (including the traditional *baba*) and coffee. The decor hasn't changed since 1830 (notice the lovely mosaic floor). Expect to pay 200F if you order à la carte. We recommend grilled cod with truffle purée, salmon or salted beef. For a special occasion order a half-litre carafe of champagne.

Aux Pains Perdus

9, Rue du 29-Juillet, 75001
☎ 01 42 61 17 07
Metro Tuileries
Open Mon.-Fri. 9am-5pm, Sun. & Sat. 10am-5pm.

After spending all your money buying jewellery at the nearby Place Vendôme, a light lunch is just what you need. Try a delicious fresh sandwich made with a baguette or one of the speciality breads. The French toasts that give the place its name are not, however, particularly tasty.

Ambassade d'Auvergne

22, Rue du Grenier-Saint-Lazare, 75003
☎ 01 42 72 31 22
Metro Étienne Marcel
Open every day noon-2pm, 7.30-10pm
À la carte 230F, gourmet menu 170F.

It's unusual to find traditional specialities from the Auvergne in a Parisian restaurant. Try this noisy, friendly place after a tour

AMBASSADE D'AUVERGNE
22 RUE
DU GRENIER
SAINT-LAZARE
75003 PARIS
TÉL. (1) 42.72.31.22
FAX (1) 42.78.85.47

of the Beaubourg. They serve filling dishes like *cassoulet* with lentils, blood sausage with chestnuts, tripe and so on.

Brin de Zinc

50, Rue Montorgueil, 75002
☎ 01 40 21 10 80
Metro Les Halles
Open Mon.-Sat. to midnight
Closed Sun.
Menu 180-250F.

This restaurant is an atmospheric place full of bric-a-brac, and has a great bar. The nightlife on this street is colourful too. Enjoy the homemade dishes, including courgette gratin.

La Mule du Pape

8, Rue du Pas-de-la-Mule, 75003
☎ 01 42 74 55 80

Metro Chemin Vert
Open Mon.-Fri. 11am-
3.30pm, 7-11pm, Sat. 11am-
midnight, Sun. 11am-7pm.
(except July and Aug.).

Enjoy brunch, lunch or dinner near the Place des Vosges in this Southern French restaurant. Large salads (55-60F), eggs Florentine or scrambled, lemon chicken, veal with herbs—there's a huge choice, and everything is homemade.

Jo Goldenberg

7, Rue des Rosiers, 75004
☎ 01 48 87 20 16
Metro St-Paul
Open every day 9am-midnight (deli to 11pm.)
Menu 150F.

There's an appetizing delicatessen in this excellent Jewish restaurant. House specialities include pastrami, beef Stroganoff, stuffed carp or smoked salmon (smoked by the restaurant). The deli sells delicious ryebreads and pumpernickels.

Mavrommatis

42, Rue Daubenton, 75005
☎ 01 43 31 17 17

MᴀᴠʀᴏᴍᴍᴀᴛɪS
le restaurant

42 rue Daubenton · 75005 Paris
Réservation : 01 43 31 17 17

Metro Censier
Open Tue.-Sun. noon-11pm.
Menu 140F, à la carte 200-250F.

This is arguably the best Greek restaurant in town. Settle comfortably into your sea-blue chair, and take your pick from

thirty *mezze* (starters). Then try the shoulder of lamb with herbs, or choose from the swordfish, mullet, or *sheftalia* (lamb). The service is charmingly Greek.

Le Square Trousseau

1, Rue Antoine Vollon 75012
☎ 01 43 43 06 00
Metro Ledru-Rollin
Open every day noon-2.30pm, 8-11.30pm.

This restaurant is located next to a charming, and very Parisian square not far from the Bastille. It has kept its original decor: mouldings on the ceiling, brown leather seats and an old bar with bevelled mirrors. The waiters wear long aprons, as in the traditional

brasseries. Often used as a film set, and a favourite spot for the local chic set. The lunchtime menu is excellent value at 135F. Dinner à la carte is around 230F per person.

Polidor

41, Rue Monsieur-le-Prince, 75005
☎ 01 43 26 95 34
Metro Luxembourg or Odéon
Open every day noon-2.30pm, 7pm-12.30am
Menu 55-100F, à la carte from 120F

The decor in this restaurant is about 150 years old. The menu includes *blanquette* of veal and *boeuf bourguignon*. Don't miss the bathroom with a mural by César Auguste.

Brasserie des Musées

49, Rue de Turenne, 75003,
☎ 01 42 72 96 17
Metro Saint-Paul
Open every day 7am-1am.

This traditional bistrot in the heart of the Marais, decorated in 1900s style, serves traditional cuisine, with provincial dishes, including sausages with lentils, quiche, calf's liver, sweetbread and sole. Main course 65-90F.

Osteria del Passe-Partout

20, Rue de l'Hirondelle, 75006
☎ 01 46 34 14 54
Metro St-Michel

Closed Sun.
Menus 86F, 94F, 130F.

It's a nice surprise to find such a great Italian restaurant so near Saint-Michel. Enjoy the rabbit and pasta dishes, and the delicious smells of basil and sage.

Le Perron

6, Rue Perronet, 75007
☎ 01 45 44 71 51
Metro Saint-Germain-des-Prés
Open every day noon-3pm,
7pm-midnight (exc. Sun. night).

Try the southern Italian specialities, such as spaghetti with crayfish or cuttlefish ink, tortellini with snails, and delicious homemade desserts. Reservations recommended.

Le Bistro Mazarin

42, Rue Mazarine, 75006
☎ 01 43 29 99 01
Metro Odéon
Open every day 8.30am-2am.
Menus 150-250F.

This classic bistrot with paper tablecloths attracts a young, trendy clientèle. You can have a meal for 130-150F, with a starter (hot goat's cheese salad, eggs mimosa),

and for a main course (*boeuf bourguignon*, veal chop, steak *au bleu*). It has a large selection of Bordeaux wines. In summer, relax on the terrace at the corner of Rue Callot.

Le Café des Lettres

53, Rue de Verneuil, 75007
☎ 01 42 22 52 17
Metro Rue du Bac
Open every day noon-3pm,

7pm-1am. Closed Sun. in summer.
Main dish 75F.

There's a relaxed atmosphere in this Scandinavian restaurant run by two Finnish women. Smoked and marinated fish specialities (herring, salmon) and fish croquettes are on the menu. Seating on the patio in fine weather.

Thoumieux

79, Rue Saint-Dominique, 75007
☎ 01 47 05 49 75
Metro Latour-Maubourg
Open every day noon-3.30pm, 6.30pm to midnight. Open all day Sun. Menu 82F.

This is a large brasserie, with excellent homemade products including specialities from the southwest, such as foie gras. The service is good and there are always regular customers.

Virgin Café

58-60, Champs-Élysées, 75008
☎ 01 42 89 46 81
Metro George V or Franklin-Roosevelt
Open every day to midnight.
À la carte 100F, brunch Sun. 84F or 125F.

This is a relaxed place, popular with young people. Enjoy a glass of wine or a good meal. Happy hour is from 5 to 7pm.

Le Clown Bar

114, Rue Amelot, 75011
☎ 01 43 55 87 35
Metro Filles du Calvaire
Open every day noon-3pm,
7pm-1am. Closed Sun. in
summer. Menu from 75F.

Next to the Cirque d'Hiver, this 1920s-style restaurant is usually busy. The menu includes hot sausage with lentils and oxtail, with a good selection of wines.

Lina's

Blvd des Italiens, 75009
☎ 01 42 46 02 06
Ave. de l'Opéra, 75009
☎ 01 47 03 30 29
Open every day 10am-
9.30pm (to 6pm on Sun.).

Join the rush to try the most fashionable sandwiches in Paris. Other locations include Rue Étienne-Marcel, Rue Marbeuf and St-Sulpice.

L'Avenue

41, Ave. Montaigne, 75008,
☎ 01 40 70 14 91
Metro Franklin-Roosevelt
Open every day 8am-midnight.
Closed Sat. & Sun. in Aug.
Á la carte 250-300F.

The interior designer Jacques Grange has given this *brasserie* a new look, more in keeping with its neighbouring fashion houses. Try a club sandwich, a 'chef's suggestion', a seafood platter, or the house speciality, snail risotto.

Colette

213, Rue Saint-Honoré, 75001
☎ 01 55 35 33 90
Metro Tuileries
Open Mon.-Sat. 10.30am-
7.30pm. Á la carte 100-150F.

This basement bar sells more than 20 varieties of bottled water, and serves good food too. Great for a light lunch if you're in the area.

Chartier

7, Rue du Faubourg
Montmartre, 75009
☎ 01 47 70 86 29
Metro Rue Montmartre
Open every day 11.30am-
3pm, 6-10pm.

More than 1,500 meals are served every day in this unique cafeteria, which has been going strong since it opened in 1896. The decor is pure 1900s, with a huge clock and a glass roof. The cuisine is traditional. Thursday's special dish of the day is pig's trotters!

SOMETHING SPECIAL

Here are some special venues to try, based on the quality of the food and atmosphere.

Le Grand Véfour

17, Rue de Beaujolais, 75001
☎ 01 42 96 56 27
Metro Palais-Royal
Closed Aug.

Here you'll find wood carvings in Louis XVI-style, 19th-century paintings inspired by Pompeian frescoes, and the table where Victor Hugo used to sit. With its view of the Palais-Royal, it is very much in demand.

La Tour d'Argent

15-17, Quai de la Tournelle 75005 ☎ 01 43 54 23 31
Metro Maubert-Mutualité
Closed Mon.

You'll have one of the most beautiful views in Paris from the bay windows which overlook Notre-Dame. You may not be able to afford it (booking advisable), but at least you know it exists.

Drouant

18, Rue Gaillon, 75002
☎ 01 42 65 15 16
Metro Opéra
Open to midnight
Menu 230 FF, à la carte 400F.

Excellent food. Don't leave without seeing the beautiful banister.

Lipp

151, Blvd Saint-Germain, 75006
☎ 01 45 48 53 91
Metro Saint-Germain-des-Prés
Open to 1am. Menu 250F.

Lipp was created in 1880 and is still worth a visit, even though the sauerkraut is not as good as it used to be. It's the favourite spot on Friday nights of the 'in' crowd, celebrities and politicians.

Le Procope

13, Rue de l'Ancienne-Comédie, 75006
☎ 01 40 46 79 00
Metro Odéon
Open every day to 1am.

This is the oldest restaurant in the capital.

Lapérouse

51, Quai des Grands-Augustins, 75006
☎ 01 43 26 90 14
Metro Saint-Michel
Open every day to 10.30pm.

Pure magic. Sit by the window.

Le Train Bleu

Gare de Lyon, 20 Blvd Diderot, 75012
☎ 01 43 43 09 06
Metro Gare de Lyon
Open every day to 10pm.

A high class *brassiere* located in the station with absolutely stunning Belle Époque decor.

Lucas-Carton

9 Pl. de la Madeleine, 75008
☎ 01 42 65 22 90
Metro Madeleine
Closed Sat. lunch & Sun.
Menu 400-1000F.

Alain Senderens' cuisine is served in a light wood panelled room.

La Closerie des Lilas

171, Blvd du Montparnasse, 75006
☎ 01 40 51 34 50
Metro Port-Royal
Open every day to 11.30pm, bar to 1am.

A favourite haunt of writers, past and present, from Henry James to Hemingway. Order a cocktail and soak up the atmosphere.

Maxim's

3, Rue Royale, 75008
☎ 01 42 65 27 94
Metro Concorde
Closed Sun. (all year) & Mon. in summer.

With its superb Art Nouveau decor, Maxim's was classified

a historical monument in 1979. Notice the glass roof, which has 180 decorative motifs, the mirrors and paintings.

Fermette Marbeuf

5, Rue Marbeuf, 75008.
☎ 01 53 23 08 00
Metro Franklin-Roosevelt
Open to 11.30pm (12.30am weekends).

For the fantastic decor in the Belle Époque room.

Specialised shopping areas

Home stores
① Rue de Paradis (crystal and tableware)
② Rue du Faubourg Saint-Antoine (furniture)
③ Place Saint-Pierre (fabrics, trimmings)
④ Rue Coquillère (tableware and kitchen supply stores)

Clothes (sales outlets)
⑤ Rue Saint-Placide
⑥ Rue d'Alésia
⑦ Rue Meslay (shoes)

Clothes (designer)
⑧ Faubourg Saint-Honoré
⑨ Avenue Montaigne, rue François-Ier

Jewellery
⑩ Place Vendôme (luxury shops)
⑪ Boulevard Barbès (North African jewellery)
⑫ Rue de Bretagne, rue des Archives (costume jewellery)

Flea Markets
⑬ Vanves flea market
⑭ Saint-Ouen flea market
⑮ Montreuil flea market
⑯ Rond-Point des Champs-Élysées, near Ave. Matignon (stamp market)

Antiques
⑰ Place du Palais-Royal, Louvre des Antiquaires
⑱ Carré Rive-Gauche
⑲ Village suisse (Avenue Suffren)

Cars, motorcycles, bicycles
⑳ Boulevard Richard-Lenoir (motorcycle equipment, accessories)
㉑ Avenue de la Grande Armée (motorcycles, bicycles and car show rooms)
㉒ Avenue des Champs-Élysées (car manufacturer show rooms)

Music
㉓ Rue de Rome (stringed instrument and sheet music)
㉔ Rue de Douai, rue Victor Massé (guitars and drums)

Miscellaneous
㉕ Boulevard Saint-Michel, Blvd. Saint-Germain (books)
㉖ Boulevard de Sébastopol (African hairdressers and hair pieces)
㉗ Avenue Daumesnil (computers)
㉘ Boulevard de Clichy (sex shops)
㉙ Quai de la Mégisserie (animals)
㉚ Rue Saint-Jacques, rue du Sommerard (specialised sports shops)

Where to shop

Ethnic areas

① Avenue de Choisy (Chinatown)
② Rue des Rosiers (Jewish quarter)
③ Rue de Belleville (North African and Asian quarters)
④ Rue du Faubourg du Temple (Turkish quarter)
⑤ Boulevard de Belleville (African quarter)
⑥ Rue du Faubourg Saint-Martin (Indian and Sri Lankan quarter)

shopping in Paris

You'll never run out of things to buy or places to shop with over 30,000 large and small shops to choose from.

OPENING HOURS

Usually 9.30-10am-6.30-7pm (department stores stay open late once a week and on Sundays for a few weeks before Christmas). Chain stores such as Monoprix and Prisunic stay open till 9 or even 10pm (to midnight on the Champs-Élysées). The Drugstore on the Champs-Élysées is open 24 hours a day.

Boutiques may close for an hour or so at lunchtime, and many close altogether for a month in the summer, usually August.

The small local grocery stores, generally run by North Africans, open early and don't close till 11 or 12pm. The prices tend to be higher than in a Monoprix, for example, but they are convenient and often the only place to buy provisions late at night.

Food stores (butchers, cheese merchants, greengrocers) usually close from 1-3pm or 4pm, as well as Sunday afternoons and Mondays, but bakers, tobacconists and chemists are usually open during lunch hours.

You can buy clothes, records, books, perfumes, jewellery, gadgets and souvenirs all day long.

SHOPPING CENTRES

A number of shopping centres have opened over the last 20 years, the Carrousel du Louvre (in the Grand Louvre, entrance at 99, Rue de Rivoli, 75001, closed Tuesdays), the Forum des Halles (entrance at the Rue Pierre Lescot or the Rue Berger, 75001, closed Sundays), and the shopping centre on the Champs-Élysées (between the traffic circle and the Rue de Berri). All have fashion boutiques, jewellers, cafés and restaurants, for wet-weather days, but they're often crowded.

AN ANCIENT TRADITION OF GUILDS

Early on, guilds of shop-keepers and craftsmen set up in specific areas of the town, a tradition which persists to this day. You'll find crystal and porcelain on the Rue de Paradis; bookshops and publishers in the vicinity of Saint-Germain-des-Prés and Odéon; furniture and hardware stores along Faubourg Saint-Antoine; musical instruments and sheet music on the Rue de Rome behind the

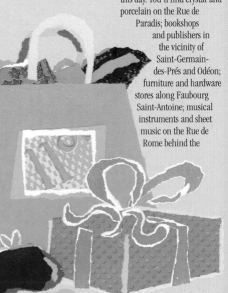

Saint-Lazare station, and on the streets leading to the Place Pigalle. Avant-garde fashion designers are at (or near) the Place des Victoires, while the world's most famous jewellers are centred on the Rue de la Paix and the Place Vendôme.

The best place to purchase fabrics is at the Marché Saint-Pierre (at the foot of the Sacré-Coeur), and several computer stores are on the Avenue Daumesnil, near the Gare de Lyon train station.

PRICES

Goods are usually priced by retailers and it's not customary to bargain in stores. But at flea markets, secondhand dealers and some antique dealers, haggling is the name of the game.

Having found the dinner service of your dreams in one of the department stores, ensure your dream does not become a nightmare.

FINDING YOUR WAY

The map references next to each of the names listed in the Shopping and Night-life chapters refer to the map on pages 80-81

Check on delivery procedures (if you paid over 1,000F and have an address near Paris, delivery is free); if you live abroad, delivery will cost extra, and you should check the transport prices.

HOW TO PAY

If you don't have cash, you can usually pay by credit card (*carte de crédit*). Generally shops and restaurants accept American Express, Diner's

Club. Mastercard (sometimes called Eurocard) and Visa, but check first with the shop or restaurant if you are in doubt.

In theory, Eurocheques can be used in France, but few shops accept them. Banks will cash them, but may insist on a minimum amount. You can use them in the larger deparment stores, however. If you don't want to keep too much cash on you, you can always go to one of the cash dispensers (ATMs) for occasional withdrawals; they're open 24 hours a day all over the capital, and have instructions in English. Your bank will usually convert at the current rate of exchange, but there will be a handling charge – usually higher than for withdrawing money at home.

Although traveller's cheques are promoted as safe and easy to use, French shopkeepers (and restaurants) are often reluctant to accept them, suggesting instead that you change them first at the nearest bank.

SHIPPING GOODS HOME

If you find the little 19th-century dressing table or Louis XVI bed that you've always wanted, you can arrange for the antique dealer to send it on to you, or organise a private carrier (cost according to volume). If you want your purchase sent abroad, it will have to be packed securely and the vendor must supply a proforma invoice for customs purposes.

RECLAIMING VAT

If you are resident outside the European community you can claim a tax refund on goods you take back home, whether physically taking them with you, or having them sent on by a forwarder. You can claim back the sales tax (VAT or *TVA*) which you pay as part of the purchase price providing you spend more than F2000 in one shop. You should ask for a *bordereau de détaxe* which you then present at customs on your departure, or send back to the shop within 3 months of purchase. The money will then be refunded to you, but be aware that it may take some time. Note that you cannot reclaim tax on certain goods, eg. food, drink or tobacco. If you are resident within the European community you cannot reclaim the tax.

Customs information:
☎ 01 40 24 65 10

QUINTESSENTIAL PARIS

There are certain places that any shopping expedition in Paris simply must include. They are not necessarily the most expensive or the most stylish, but they reveal the essence of the capital and what it does best. Here are just a few of the shops.

Guerlain

68, Av. des Champs-Élysées, 75008 (A3)
☎ **01 45 62 52 57**
Metro Franklin D. Roosevelt
Open Mon.-Sat. 9.45am-7pm, Sun. 3-7pm.

This is undoubtably the most beautiful perfume shop in Paris, with its original 1912 decor of marble and mirrors. You'll discover all the most famous perfumes, with evocative names such as *Shalimar*, *Chamade*, *l'Heure Bleue*, *Jardin de Bagatelle* and *Champs-Élysées*.

Benetton

75, Blvd Malesherbes, 75008. (B3)
☎ **01 43 87 57 39**
Metro Saint-Augustin

Open Mon.-Fri. 9am-6.15pm, Sat. 9am-noon. Closed Sun.

This family business was founded in 1880 in Paris, and it's one of the few surviving engraving businesses. The interior is like a 19th-century chemist or an old fashioned gentleman's club. Formal embossed cards, with gouache borders or floral and animal prints, cost 19F each, with a matching envelope, 180F for 10 and 685F for 50. You can also order personalised cards. This shop has nothing to do with Italian sweaters!

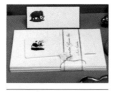

Angélina

226, Rue de Rivoli, 75001 (C3)
☎ **01 42 60 82 00**
Metro Tuileries
Open every day 9am-7pm.

This old-fashioned tearoom is the ideal spot to relax after a visit to the Louvre or a walk through the Tuileries. Try their unbeatable hot chocolate, *l'Africain*, which costs 36F and is famous throughout Paris. You should choose a *Mont Blanc* to go with it, a meringue cake with Chantilly and chestnut cream (36F). You can also buy chocolates here.

Poilâne

8, Rue du Cherche-Midi, 75006 (B4)
☎ **01 45 48 42 59**
Metro Sevres-Babylone
Open every day (exc. Sun.) 7.15am-8pm.

Parisians love Poilâne. This bakery opened in 1936 and owes its reputation to its famous unleavened bread, which is baked in a wood fire. It will last a week if you keep it wrapped up. You can have it delivered right to your door, anywhere in France, if you fill in an order form. For 40F, including delivery, you too can enjoy Monsieur Poilâne's bread for breakfast.

Androüet

6, Rue Arsene Housssaye, 75008 (B2)
☎ **42 89 95 00**
Metro Liège
Open Tue.-Sat. 10am-8pm.

Cheese lovers and connoisseurs will find themselves in paradise in this highly acclaimed shop. It boasts 150 varieties, including classics such as Camembert and Sainte-Maure, and more unusual varieties such as Lou Picadou, a goat's cheese rolled in paper. Delightful wooden boxes make original gifts, at 160F for 6 cheeses, 300F for 12, but do take care to store them in a cool place.

Ladurée
16, Rue Royale, 75008 (B3)
☎ 01 42 60 21 79
Metro Madeleine
Mon.-Sat. 8.30am-7pm,
Sun. 10am-7pm.
Closed Sun. in summer.

This Parisian institution is a sophisticated tearoom with a very

chic clientèle. It's famous throughout France for its magnificent macaroons. They come in all flavours, including coffee, chocolate, pistachio and vanilla. Take-away macaroons are 17F each, and they keep up to 4 or 5 days in the fridge.

À la Mère de Famille
35, Rue du Faubourg,
Montmartre, 75009 (C3)
☎ 01 47 70 83 69
Metro Le Peletier
Open Tue.-Fri. 8.30am-
1.30pm, 3-7pm, Sat.
8.30am-12.30pm, 3-7pm
Closed Aug.

This is without doubt one of the most beautiful shops in Paris. It has a turn of the century interior with blue and white tiles, and serves traditional confectionery from the provinces. Sugared almonds, shortbread biscuits and madeleines will tempt you, but not as much as their famous *délice de mer*. This consists of chocolate, covered in a rum and raisin flavoured almond paste and is only for those with a very sweet tooth. You can buy a selection of regional liqueurs, including aged Armagnac (262F) or Calvados (173F).

La Civette
157, Rue Saint-Honoré,
75001 (C3)
☎ 01 42 96 04 99
M Palais-Royal-Musée
du Louvre
Open every day (exc. Sun.)
9.30am-7pm.

Parisian smokers love La Civette. It sells tobacco, cigars, beautiful pipes and all the accessories that go with them, including the humidor, which is a cigar box equipped with a humidifier (1100F). Cigars from Cuba, Domingo and Honduras cost between 13-130F each. A box of 25 starts at 190F.

AND DON'T MISS:

Barthélémy, the other great Parisian cheese store (51, Rue de Grenelle, 75007, A4 ☎ 01 42 22 82 24); **Berthillon,** THE Parisian ice-cream shop, for unbeatable sorbet (see p. 59); **Mariage Frères** for a selection of teas (see p. 108) ; **Hédiard,** for crystallized fruits (see p. 36); **Verlet** for coffee (see p. 109); **Lachaume** for cut flowers and bouquets (10, rue Royale, 75008, B3 ☎ 01 42 60 57 26); **Dalloyau,** for exceptional croissants at the Place du Luxembourg from 8.30am (2, Pl. Edmond Rostand, 75006, C4 ☎ 01 43 29 31 10).

WOMEN'S FASHION

Parisian women seem to have an innate sense of style, enabling them to dress at the height of fashion without succumbing to the more outlandish vagaries of street style. The streets of Saint-Germain and the Marais are full of fashion boutiques providing ample inspiration for achieving that chic, French look, from the classic little black number to an elegant bag or smart accessories. *Allez, les filles!*

CLOTHES

Gap

14, Rue Lobineau, 75006 (C4)
☎ 01 44 32 07 30
Metro Odéon or
St.-Germain-des-Prés
Open Mon.-Sat. 10am-8pm.

New stock arrives from the States every six weeks and the previous collection is sold off. Jeans, jackets, and sportswear. Shirts cost from 145 to 200F.

Schinichiro Arakawa

1, Rue du Plâtre, 75004 (C4)
☎ 01 42 78 24 21
Metro Hôtel de Ville
Open Tue.-Sat., 11am-
7.30pm.

This fantastic boutique is the perfect setting for the latest creations by this up-and-coming Japanese designer. This is the only place in France where you can find Ian Reeds' amazing shoes or the photo magazine, *Zine 3*. T-shirts at 230-400F and dresses at 1500F are available.

Loft

12, Rue du Faubourg Saint-
Honoré, 75008 (B3)
☎ 01 42 65 59 65
Metro Madeleine
56, Rue de Rennes, 75006
☎ 01 45 44 88 99
Metro Saint-Germain-des-Prés
Open Mon.-Sat. 10am-7pm.

New York warehouse-style decor and reasonable prices. Sports shirts, shirts, T-shirts, all sold in cloth bags. The style is contemporary and natural. Trousers cost 600F and shirts 345F.

Lolita Lempicka

14, Rue du Fg. Saint-Honoré,
75008 (B3)
☎ 01 49 24 94 01
Metro Madeleine or Concorde
Open Mon.-Sat. 10.30am-7pm.

Come here for a theatrical and glamourous look. You'll find slim-fitting suits and dresses with a touch of lace, a trace of transparency, a hint of pink, and evening dress from 4,000F. Also at 46 Ave. Victor Hugo (75016).

Studio Lolita

2, Rue des Rosiers, 75004 (D4)
☎ 01.48.87.09.67.
Open Tue.-Sun. 10.30am-
1pm, 2.30-7pm.

See past collections here.

SYTHETIC FABRICS

How much do you know about artificial and synthetic fabrics? Artificial fabrics such as viscose, acetate or modal are made from a cellulose pulp derived from conifers or broad-leaved trees like beech or birch. Synthetic fabrics (polyamide, polyester, acrylic) are made from a petroleum derivative known as naphtha. The chemical transformation of the raw material creates the strands which are made into thread, and then used to weave synthetic fabrics.

The clothes and colours come all the way from India. You'll find cashmere cotton in a range of warm Indian reds, yellows and oranges. The Nehru jacket is a popular design and the silk trousers are to die for (from 850F).

Être Ronde en Couleurs

1, Rue de Rivoli, 75004 (D4)
☎ 01 48 04 56 57
Metro St Paul
Open Mon.-Sat. 10.30am-7pm, Thur. & Fri. to 7.30pm.

This is the place for women with a fuller figure. It has lovely lingerie and evening wear.

Martin Grant

32, Rue des Rosiers, 75004 (D4)

☎ 01 42 71 39 49
Metro St Paul
Open Tue.-Sun. 11am-7.30pm.

Once a Jewish barbershop, this is now an Australian fashion house. This is the only place you'll find his superb crêpes de Chine and stunning gauzes. Dresses cost from 1500F.

Les Mariées de Lolita

15, Rue Pavée, 75004 (D4)
☎ 01 48 04 96 96
Open every day, visits by appointment. Closed in Aug.

Wonderful collections in lace and taffeta.

Maria

28, Rue Pierre Lescot, 75001 (C3)
☎ 01 40 13 06 00
Metro Étienne Marcel
Open Mon.-Sat., 10.30am-7.30pm.

The exclusive creations here include superb backless dresses in tactel (just like a second skin) from 790-1490F. There's a selection of 30 tops that are really unique, some simple, others with lace (200-400F).

Mohanjeet

21, Rue Saint-Sulpice, 75006 (C4)
☎ 01 43 54 73 29
Metro Odéon
Open Mon. 2-7pm, Tue.-Sat. 10.30am-7pm.

Doria Salambo

38, Rue de la Roquette, 75011 (D4)
☎ 01 47 00 06 30
Metro Bastille
Open Mon. 2-8pm, Tue.-Sat. 11am-8pm.

Doria creates her own styles and fabrics. She can also adapt them to your taste. Suits cost from 700-800F.

Sunshine

48, Rue de Rivoli, 75004 (C4)
☎ 01 42 72 02 50
Metro Hôtel de Ville
172, Rue du Temple, 75003 (D3)
☎ 01 48 04 55 20
Metro Temple
Open Mon.-Sat. 9.30am-7pm.

This shop has all sorts of things at all sorts of prices, including skirts for 200F, 70s style trousers or hound's-tooth suits.

LINGERIE

Comme des Femmes

31, Rue St Placide, 75006 (B4)
☎ 01 45 48 97 33
Metro St Placide
Open Tue.-Sat. 10am-7pm, Mon. from 11am.

A Parisian soirée in inappropriate underwear is simply unthinkable. You'll find what you need here, at attractive prices. All the big name lingerie is here at 30-50% less than elsewhere, plus a wide range of tights for winter. Come here for your swimsuits in summer.

SHIRTS

Big Ben Club

72, Rue Bonaparte, 75006 (B4)
☎ 01 40 46 02 12
Metro Saint-Sulpice
Open Mon.-Sat. 10.30am-7pm.

This was the first shop in Paris to specialise in white blouses, and it's become an institution. Choose from cotton piqué or pure cotton, in more than 80 styles (295-395F).

Anne Fontaine

64, 66, Rue des Saints-Pères, 75007 (B4)
☎ 01 45 48 89 10
Metro Saint-Germain-des-Prés
Open Mon.-Sat. 10.30am-2pm, 3-7pm.
50, Rue Étienne-Marcel, 75002 (C3)
☎ 01 40 41 08 32
Metro Étienne Marcel
Open Mon.-Sat. 10.30am-2pm, 3-7pm.

Anne Fontaine sells shirts and blouses in immaculate white cottons and poplins. Pretty buttons and cuffs demonstrate a special attention to detail. You can also buy pretty, sheer waistcoats. Many styles, from 395F.

BAGS AND ACCESSORIES

Swatch Store

10, Rue Royale, 75008 (B3)
☎ 01 42 60 58 38
Metro Concorde
Open Mon.-Sat. 9.30am-7pm.

You'll find the whole range of Swatch watches here, and much more besides. For an annual subscription of 500F, you can join the *Swatch Collector's* club, which entitles you to a collector's watch every year and a guide to all the previous designs. You'll also be given the secret code to access a Swatch swap service.

Totale Éclipse

40, Rue de la Roquette, 75011 (D4)
☎ 01 48 07 88 04
Metro Bastille
Open Mon.-Sat. 11am-7.30pm.

Glass, ceramic and silver-plated jewellery in original and unusual designs. The more classic creations come in a range of four basic colours. Necklaces and rings start at 65F, and there are some tempting bags.

Upla

17, Rue des Halles, 75001 (C3)
☎ 01 40 26 49 96
Metro Châtelet
Open Mon.-Sat. 10.30am-1.30pm, 2-7pm.

Upla's plastic-coated canvas

pouch-bag, with its practical pockets has become famous (610-2,000F). Now they also offer a range of shirts, jumpers and soft leather bags in four colours.

HATS

Axes et Soirs

97, Rue Vieille-du-Temple, 750003 (D4)
☎ 01 42 74 13 62
Metro Saint-Paul
Open Mon.-Fri. 10am-7pm, Sat. 11am-7pm.

Two inspired milliners make these stylish original hats. Their made-to-measure designs cost almost the same as ready-to-wear, so you can bring your own fabric along too. About 1,000F each.

Marie Mercié

56, Rue Tiquetonne, 75002 (C3)
☎ 01 40 26 60 68
Metro Étienne Marcel
23, Rue Saint-Sulpice, 75006 (C4)
☎ 01 43 26 45 83
Metro Odéon
Open Mon.-Sat. 11am-7pm.

Marie works magic, with a touch of poetry and humour. She's as clever with straw as she is with velvet. Plenty of scope for the daring, you could come away wearing a bird on your head, or even an admiral's hat! She has two collections a year, with hats from 900F.

SOCKS AND TIGHTS

Bleu-Forêt

33, Rue des Petits-Champs, 75002 (C3)
☎ 01 40 20 00 17
Metro Palais-Royal-Musée du Louvre
Open Mon.-Fri. 9.30am-3pm, 4-6pm.
59, Rue de Rennes, 75006 (B4)
☎ 01 45 48 27 46
Metro Saint-Sulpice
Open Tue.-Fri. 10am-7pm, Sat. 9.30am-7.30pm.

Cotton, linen or wool, plain or patterned, these socks are made to be seen. Classic and sporty tights and women's socks are available from 55F.

SHOES

Mosquitos

25, Rue du Four, 75006 (C4)
☎ 01 43 25 25 16
Metro Mabillon
Open Mon.-Sat. 10am-7.30pm
19, Rue Pierre Lescot, 75001 (C3)
☎ 01 45 08 44 72
Metro Les Halles
Open Mon.-Sat. 10am-7pm.

This shop' name is as original at its shoes. A good range including some multi-coloured designs (from 395-1,450F).

Free Lance

22, Rue Mondétour, 75001 (C3)
☎ 01 42 33 74 70
Metro Les Halles or Étienne-Marcel
Open Mon.-Fri. 10am-7pm, Sat. 10am-7.30pm.

The shoes here are always in tune with the current fashion. Designs are classic or original, flat or with heels, for all ages. There are trainers from 280 to 400F, shoes from 1000F and boots around 1500F.

Camper

25, Rue du Vieux-Colombier, 75006 (B4)
☎ 01 45 48 22 00
Metro Saint-Sulpice
Open Mon.-Sat. 10am-7pm.

If the left shoe and right shoe don't match, then they must be Camper! The Mix collection is urban-techno and made of

futuristic materials (nylons and leathers). The *Cartujana de Espana* is another Camper shoe design, which is ultra-comfortable and comes in various colours. Prices start from around 550F.

MEN'S FASHION

Along with the Italians, French men probably have the reputation for being the best dressed men in Europe. They certainly take their appearance very seriously. You'll have ample opportunity of acquiring a little of that French chicness yourself in the city's many boutiques. There is even a vogue for le style anglais, though you won't necessarily want to go home with a pair of brogues.

Lionel Nath

7, Rue Béranger, 75003 (D3)
☎ 01 48 87 81 30
Metro République
Open Mon.-Sat., 9am-6.30pm.

Take advantage of direct sales from a designer-manufacturer, who hasn't raised his prices for the last 5 years, with a wide choice of 70% wool suits for 1000F and 100% wool for 1400F.

Choose from summer jackets in microfibre for 700F, or pure cashmere winter ones for 1500F.

Anthony Peto

56, Rue Tiquetonne, 75002 (C3)
☎ 01 42 21 47 15
Metro Étienne-Marcel
Open Mon.-Sat. 11am-7pm.

If you just must have a snakeskin beret or a black fez with a red

pompon, this is definitely the place to come. If you prefer a bowler, Panama or cap, you'll still be spoilt for choice. Fedoras start at 600F and top hats at 980F and up.

Brummell

61, Rue Caumartin, 75009 (B3)
☎ 01 42 82 50 00
Metro Havre-Caumartin
Open Mon.-Sat. 9.30am-7pm, Thur. to 10pm.

Part of the Printemps department store is named after the famous Englishman. A menswear shop with all the major names and styles, it sells classic, sportswear and more unusual clothes, from underwear in the basement to suits on the fourth floor. The 'Brummell' collection comes out twice a year, and has elegant clothes at a reasonable price.

Smuggler

Village Royal,
25, Rue Royale, 75008 (B3)
☎ 01 42 66 01 31
Metro Madeleine
64, Rue Bonaparte, 75006
☎ 01 46 34 72 29
Metro Saint-Sulpice (C4)
Open Mon. 2-7.30pm,
Tue.-Sat. 10.30am-1pm, 2-7.30pm.

With more than 400 fabrics, Smuggler specialises in made-to-measure suits, which cost just about the same as the ones in the ready-to-wear collection. You'll find Mao collars, original buttons, trousers with or without pleats. Made-to-measure clothes take two weeks. You'll pay 1960F for a 100% wool suit. This is the place to find the cheapest Alden shoes in Paris.

Le Shop

3, Rue d'Argout, 75002 (C3)
☎ 01 40 28 95 94
Metro Étienne Marcel
Open Mon. 1-7pm, Tue.-Sat. 11am-7pm.

The theme here is 'world culture', with new styles to go with techno music, house, rap and acid jazz. Have a look at their shoes and jackets, T-shirts and dungarees, Northwave shoes and Airwork trainers. Visit the brasserie for a quick snack. Internet access is available. You'll also find secondhand clothes and bikes, trousers from 300 to 600F and shirts from 250 to 500F.

Latino Rock

15, Rue de la Grande Truanderie, 75001 (C3)
☎ 01 45 08 17 01
Metro Les Halles
Open Mon.-Sat. 11am-7.30pm.

Whether you're young or not-so-young, you'll love the reefer jackets (1,200F). Try a PVC one (799F) for a change of style, plus tight-fitting T-shirts or satin shirts to wear with all kinds of suits (1400- 2200F), and beautiful Jourdan Bis shoes.

SHOES

Anatomica

14, Rue du Bourg-Tibourg, 75004 (D4)
☎ 01 42 74 10 20
Metro St Paul-le-Marais
Open Mon.-Sat. 10.30am-7.30pm, Sun. 3-7.30pm.

Anatomica sells 'shoes the shape of your feet' in classic styles. You'll find the widest selection of Birkenstock shoes in France (320-550F), plus Australian Blundstone boots

(740F) and Trippen clogs (490-640F). Try the restyled turn of the century work clothes, especially the Largeot trousers.

Sagone

44-46, Ave. de la République, 75011 (D3)
☎ 01 49 29 92 83
Metro Parmentier
Open Mon.-Sat. 10am-7.30pm.

If you have a hard time finding shoes for extra-large feet, try this wonderful

shop with its huge stock of sizes and styles. You'll find shoes for every day, for the evening, or even to get married in (400-1500F) Larger sizes for women are also available. A great place to come for those with difficult feet.

Timberland

52, Rue Croix-des-Petits-Champs, 75001 (C3)
☎ 01 45 08 41 40
Metro Palais-Royal
Open Tue.-Sat. 10.30-7pm, Mon. from 11am.

Come here for shoes and clothes made of waterproof leather, specially designed for the outdoor life. They're made of natural fabrics, like linen and cotton, in warm orange, russet and brown colours that remind you of Canadian forests. Timberland was the first manufacturer of round-toed boots with padded ankles (1150F a pair). Shirts start at 450F.

Fenestrier

23, Rue du Cherche-Midi,
75006 (B4)
☎ 01 42 22 66 02
Metro Saint-Sulpice
Open Mon.-Fri. 11am-7pm,
Sat. 10am-7pm.

Dark colours tend to be favoured at
'Fenestrier'. The designs are
classic, but there's also a younger
line of two-tone leather and canvas
shoes with rubber soles. The
summer lines include handmade
canvas shoes and sandals, with
prices from 800F.

TIES

Cravatterie Nazionali

249, Rue Saint-Honoré,
75001 (B3)
☎ 01 42 61 50 39
Metro Concorde or
Madeleine
Open Mon.-Sat. 10am-7pm.

This shop has an impressive
selection of 5,000 ties, (from 20
labels), and silk Cravatterie own
label ties from 295F. A staggering
600 styles are displayed in
wooden cabinets, and you're free
to explore the drawers and take
your pick.

Jean-Charles de Castelbajac

6, Pl. Saint-Sulpice,
75006 (C4)
☎ 01 46 33 87 32
Metro Saint-Sulpice
Open Mon.-Sat. 10am-7pm.

Castelbajac likes fun ties,
especially silk ones with woven
and relief patterns. Moons, suns,
stars and hearts are the designer's
favourite motifs. You'll find reds
and yellows, lovely beiges and
greys, as well as beautiful navys
(from 400F).

SHIRTS

Le Fou du Roi

55-57, Rue de Vaugirard,
75006 (B4)
☎ 01 45 44 07 82
Metro Rennes
Open Tue.-Sat. 10.30am-
7.30pm, Mon. noon-
7.30pm.

Stand out in a crowd, with one of
these shirts. They're multicoloured
and well-cut. A poplin shirt costs
250F, and you'll also find silk
and linen ones which are very
comfortable in the summer. There
are beautiful silk ties (150-230F),
silk waistcoats (390F) and superb
suits (cupro, linen, viscose,
velvet or microfibre) from 1250F
to 2250F.

Bain Plus

51, Rue des
Francs Bourgeois,
75004 (D4)
☎ 01 48 87 83 07
Metro Saint-Paul
Open Tue.-Sat.
11am-7:30pm,
Sun 2-7pm.

Try their herringbone
shirts, so soft you want to
sleep in them, flannelette
for winter and seersucker
poplin for summer.
An exclusive
handmade
collection of
pyjamas (from 580F),

underwear and dressing gowns
are also on sale, with matching
slippers and wash bags.

WAISTCOATS

Favour Brook

**Le Village Royal,
25, Rue Royale, 75008 (B3)
☎ 01 40 17 06 72
Metro Madeleine
Open Mon.-Sat. 10am-7pm.**

Favour Brook creates 18th-century waistcoats, with a touch of English eccentricity, in cotton and printed velvet brocades with silk embroidery. There are over 300 ready-to-wear waistcoats plus 2,000 fabrics from which to make your choice for made-to-measure (1400-2400F). Jackets with Nehru collars cost 4000F and tail coats and morning coats from 4500F. A new women's shop, *Violet by Favour Brook*, is across the street with dresses for 3000F.

LEATHER

Michel Lipsic

**52, Rue Croix-des-Petits-Champs, 75001 (C3)
☎ 01 40 41 97 47
Metro Palais-Royal-Musée du Louvre
Open Mon.-Sat. 10am-7pm.**

Their attractive pale-blue or apple-green shirts in washable Indian leather are in big demand.

You'll find all the great classics here, the safari jacket Clark Gable wore in *Mogambo*, Marlon Brando's jacket in *On the Waterfront*, plus made-to-measure clothes for the same price as ready-to-wear. There is an on-the-spot workshop for alterations, more than ten different qualities of leather in a vast range of colours. Trousers start from 2400F.

Le carreau du temple

**Rue Dupetit-Thouars and Rue Perrée, 75003 (D3)
Metro Temple
Open Tue.-Sun. 9am-1pm, Sat. to 6.30pm.**

Impecunious Parisians have been shopping for clothes under this glass roof for over 200 years, and even if the prices have changed, the tradition of bargaining remains. Try your hand at it if you find the leather jacket of your dreams (there's a wide selection, with prices from around 1,000F). There are also specialist stores worth a visit in the Rue Dupetit-Thouars.

CHILDREN'S CLOTHES AND TOYS

Paris has clothes to suit every child (and parent or grandparent) at all price ranges. You can buy casual T-shirts and jeans or cute little smocked dresses. Many designers of adult clothes now have children's ranges too, though not at insignificant prices. Toys and games are likely to be cheaper and can be a good introduction to French.

La Cerise sur le Gâteau

82, Rue de la Victoire, 75009 (C3)
☎ **01 44 53 98 89**
Metro Chaussee d'Antin
Open Tue.-Sat. 10am-7pm.
The fabrics are of top quality, the

cut excellent and the designs both original and classic. The 'cherry on the cake' in the name of the shop refers to their reversible summer and winter outfits. Girls' dresses (0-16 years) range from 100-200F with boys' trousers (0-12 years) starting at 80F.

Chattawak

5, Rue Vavin, 75006 (B4)
☎ **01 40 46 85 64**
Metro Vavin
Open Mon.-Sat. 10am-7pm.

You'll find a wide range of children's clothes for boys and girls. There's a very smart sportswear collection in red, blue and white, and clothes in very soft and comfortable fabrics that are also hard-wearing. Sweatshirts cost 85F and lycra jeans 326F.

Lara et les Garçons

60, Rue Saint-Placide, 75006 (B4)
☎ **01 45 44 01 89**
Metro Saint-Placide
Open Tue.-Sat. 10am-7pm, Mon., noon-7pm.

This shop has a constant stock of designer seconds, both clothes and shoes, for children aged 0-16. There are lots of pretty dresses starting at 89F and trousers from 59F.

Poême

71, Av. P. Doumer, 75016
☎ **01 45 03 10 33**
Metro La Muette
Open Mon.-Sat. 10.30am-1.30pm, 2.30pm-7pm.

If nothing but the best will do, this is the place to go. The Molli range caters for newborns and toddlers up to 2 years old. Poême also has clothes for 2-12 year olds, with a selection of pinafore dresses and dungarees together with more formal clothes. They have a lovely pink or red silk dress with a velvet collar and puff sleeves for 725F.

Si Tu Veux

68, Galerie Vivienne, 75002 (C3)
☎ **01 42 60 59 97**
Metro Bourse
Open Mon.-Sat. 10.30am-7pm.

This is a treasure trove of creative and imaginative gifts for children. Almost everything comes in kit form, such as fancy dress outfits either to make yourself (160-180F) or ready-made (250-300F). They have party kits in different themes, including ghosts and the circus, craft kits and even cooking kits for budding chefs.

CROISSANT

3, Rue St Merri, 75004
☎ **01 48 87 32 88**
Metro Hôtel-de-Ville
**Open Mon.-Sat. 11am-
1.30pm, 2.30-7pm.**

It's like being in a doll's house, where everything looks good enough to eat. Croissant has been making its own designs for 20 years, and has built up a loyal clientèle. The shelves are full of handmade baby clothes together with a good selection of clothes for children up to 8 years old.

Jeux Descartes

52, Rue des Écoles, 75005 (C4)
☎ **01 43 26 79 83 .**
Metro Cluny-La Sorbonne
**Open Mon. 11am-7pm,
Tue.-Sat. 10am-7pm.**

This shop will get your brain ticking with its puzzles, role-play games (50-500F) and strategic thinking games. You'll find tarot

cards and card games from all over the world, plus billiards and backgammon.

Multicubes

5, Rue de Rivoli, 75004 (D4)
☎ **01 42 77 10 77**
Metro Saint-Paul
Open Tue.-Sat. 10am-7pm.

The place to buy natural or painted wooden puppets and spinning tops, puzzles and parlour games. All kinds of things for a child's bedroom. Multicubes is also one of the few places where you'll still find Steiff cuddly toys. You'll pay about 100F for a puppet, and 200F for a height chart.

Bazar

**Royal Rivoli, 78 Rue
de Rivoli, (C4)**
☎ **01 42 72 68 79**
Metro Hôtel de Ville
**Open Mon.-Sat. 9am-
7.30pm, Sun. from 10am.**

This is a real bazaar. Cuddly toys for tiny tots, puzzles for big brothers and sisters (from 25F).

Bonpoint

**86, Rue de l'Université,
75007 (B3)**
☎ **01 45 51 46 28**
Metro Solférino
Open Mon.-Sat. 10am-7pm.
(see p. 45).

Score Games

**56, Blvd Saint-Michel,
75006 (C4)**
☎ **01 43 25 85 55**
Metro Cluny-La Sorbonne
**Open Mon. noon-7pm,
Tue.-Sat. 10am-7pm**
**46, rue des Fossés-Saint-
Bernard, 75005 (C4)**
☎ **01 53 32 03 20**
Metro Jussieu
Open Mon.-Sat. 10am-7pm.

Computer games galore, new and secondhand games with discounts of 30-80% on some. All can be refunded, returned or exchanged.

Paying in Paris

Paying can take two operations. Goods are wrapped while you pay at the *caisse*, then you collect them brandishing your receipt.

INTERIOR DESIGN

Paris has absolutely everything you could imagine or want for the home. There is a huge selection of shops brimming with ideas on how to improve your décor or add a touch of Parisian chic. The back streets of Saint-Germain-des-Pres and the Latin Quarter are full of small boutiques. Just walking around these should give you ample inspiration.

Globe Trotter
5, Rue de Medicis, 75006 (C4)
☎ 01 43 26 28 66
Metro Odeon
Open Tue.-Sat. 10.30am-7.30pm, Mon. 2-7pm.

This shop is just opposite the Luxembourg Gardens and looks more like a secondhand store,

with goods overflowing onto the pavement. The colourful furniture looks as if it has come straight from a country house in Southern France, and you'll find pedestal tables, pretty single flower vases in glass and wrought-iron (from 230FF) and other lovely pieces from Provence. Original and unique handcrafted designs are available, and there's a mail-order catalogue.

Avant-Scène
4, Pl. de l'Odéon, 75006 (C4)
☎ 01 46 33 12 40

Metro Odéon
Open Tue.-Sat. 10.30am-1pm, 2-7.30pm. Closed Aug.

Come here for some very innovative ideas (see p. 48).

Conceptua
9, Rue de la Roquette, 75011 (D4)
☎ 01 43 38 68 87

Metro Bastille
Open Mon.-Sat. 10am-7.30pm,
Sun. 2-7.30pm.

This large store is a treasure trove of original items at affordable prices. Wrought-iron mirrors for 249F, sofa beds from 1190F, contemporary-style clothes stands for 495F, lamps for 249F, ready-made curtains for 395F.

Despalles
Village Royal, 26, Rue Boissy-d'Anglas, 75008 (B3)
☎ 01 49 24 05 65
Metro Madeleine
Open Mon.-Sat. 10am-7pm, (see p. 36).

Plants and garden items as well as furniture and gifts can be found in this interesting shop (see p. 36).

Maison de Famille
29, Rue Saint-Sulpice, 75006 (C4)
☎ 01 40 46 97 47
Metro Saint-Sulpice or Odéon
Open Mon.-Sat. 10.30am-7pm.

AGNÈS COMAR

7, Ave. George-V,
75008 (A3)
☎ 01 49 52 01 89
Metro Alma-Marceau
Open Tue.-Sat. 10.30am-
1pm, 2-7pm, Mon. 2-7pm.

A marvellous store, with a charm all of its own selling elegant items in silk, linen and cotton for the living room, dining room and bedroom. You'll also find an abundance of gift ideas at reasonable prices. Silk sheets are sold in a pouch for 190F; shantung cushions filled with potpourri cost 320F and linen tablecloths are 780F.

Linen, crockery, glassware for the home, as well as good gift ideas (see p. 48).

Le Cèdre Rouge Côté Maison

25, Rue Duphot, 75008 (B3)
☎ 01 42 61 81 81
Metro Madeleine
Open Mon. noon-7pm,
Tue.-Sat 10am-7pm.

Cèdre Rouge is full of warm, sunset colours from Southern France. Many hand-made items from craftsmen working in wrought-iron, ceramic and rattan. There is also some beautiful crockery and pretty household linen as well as items such as ceramic salad-bowls (125F) and elegant wrought-iron chairs (780F).

The Conran Shop

117, Rue du Bac, 75007 (B4)
☎ 01 42 84 10 01
Metro Sèvres-Babylone
Open Mon. noon-7pm,
Tue.-Sat. 10am-7pm.

This shop is owned by the British design guru Terence Conran, so if you haven't had the opportunity to sample his choice of wares at home, nows your chance. It's the ultimate lifestyle store, where every object is a delight for the eyes, if not for the purse. There are rugs, fabrics, crockery, lights, glassware (9-155F), plates (16-170F) and vases (70-2000F). Admire the window displays, even if you don't venture in. Francophile Conran's Habitat chain is also now a fixture in French shopping malls.

Mis en Demeure

27, Rue du Cherche-Midi,
75006 (B4)
☎ 01 45 48 83 35
Metro Sèvres-Babylone
Open Mon. 1-7.30pm,
Tue.-Sat. 10am-7.30pm.

This is a modern shop, despite the nostalgic appeal of its furniture. You'll find ideas for the kitchen and bedroom in soft colours. Turned wood, cut glass, embroidered cushions, printed cotton tablemats (95F) or an antiqued extending table (6250F).

Contrepoint

59, Rue de Seine, 75006 (C4)
☎ 01 40 51 88 98

Metro Mabillon
Open Mon.-Sat. 10am-7pm.

Started by a fabric designer who decided to go into interior decoration, this is a bright and cheerful shop, with an inspirational mail-order catalogue. There are very comfortable armchairs and sofas, pretty crockery, pottery and lampshades. Goods can be made to order, with professional advice.

DECORATION, TABLEWARE AND DESIGN

Tableware is an important element in home decoration for the French and they pay great attention to the presentation of the table when entertaining, from choice of cutlery and glasses to the folding of napkins. There are many shops in Paris specialising in this area and new collections come out twice a year. They often include unique, original and sometimes even limited designs for special occasions or for everyday use. Here are a few of the best places to go.

Bodum Shop

99, Rue de Rivoli, Carrousel du Louvre, 3, Allée de Rivoli 75001 (C3)
☎ 01 42 60 47 11
Metro Palais-Royal-Musée du Louvre
Open every day 11am-8pm, Tue. 12.30-7.30pm.

Bodum invented the plunge cafetière and teapot. Most of the items in the collection are simple and practical, with many Danish designs in wood. Pepper and salt mills, nutcrackers, breadboards, bottle racks, distinctive glass and wooden jars. Teapots cost from 115 to 500F.

Dîners en Ville

27, Rue de Varenne 75007 (B4)
☎ 01 42 22 78 33
Metro Rue du Bac
Open Mon. 2-7pm, Tue.-Sat. 11am-7pm.

Bright colours dominate this store, with printed tablecloths by Gérard Danton, Beauvillé, and Jacquard. There are also Portuguese plates in vivid colours and cutlery with multi-coloured, mother-of-pearl or transparent handles (from 130F per piece). Glasses are from 60-200F each.

Kitchen Bazaar

11, Ave du Maine 75014 (B5)
☎ 01 42 22 91 17
Metro Montparnasse-Bienvenüe.
Galerie des Trois Quartiers 23, Blvd de la Madeleine 75001 (B3)
☎ 01 42 60 50 30
Metro Madeleine
Open Mon.-Sat. 10am-7pm.

For 30 years, Kitchen Bazaar has created new designs using modern materials, in particular stainless steel. They sell kitchen utensils which are as beautiful as they are useful, manufactured in the USA or in Japan, and definitely made to be seen. Stainless-steel toasters cost 350F.

Laure Japy

36, Rue du Bac, 75007 (B4)
☎ 01 42 86 96 97
Metro Rue du Bac
Open Mon.-Sat. 10.30am-7pm.

Everything here is made to mix and match, including the Limoges china services. There are two collections a year, with new styles, patterns, colours and a selection of glassware, cutlery, tablecloths and tablemats.

À la Mine d'Argent

108, Rue du Bac 75007(B4)
☎ 01 45 48 70 68
Metro Rue du Bac
Open Mon.-Fri. 10am-7pm,
Sat. 11am-6pm.

The is the ideal shop for antique silverware, both silver plate and

solid silver. You can buy one item or a whole set. It's a true gold mine if you're looking for the odd item of cutlery. There's even a silversmith on the spot, who makes classic designs at very reasonable prices. You can bring in silver for all kinds of repairs, including silver-plating, embossing and engraving.

La Tisanière

21, Rue de Paradis 75010 (C3)
☎ 01 47 70 22 80
Metro Poissonnière
Open Mon.-Sat. 9.45am-6.30pm, Sat. to 6.15pm.

This shop sells white china crockery which you can decorate yourself, if you prefer the personal touch

(plates from 20F). If your taste leans more towards traditional designs, you'll find copies of famous French 18th-century porcelain (plates from 65F) plus glassware and cutlery too.

Décors et Transparences

97, Rue du Bac 75007 (B4)
☎ 01 45 48 95 39
Metro Rue du Bac
Open Mon. 2-7pm,
Tue.-Sat. 11am-7pm.

Lights and other items made by master glass craftsmen from the island of Murano in Italy. Also available are Florentine glasses, in rich warm Italian colours, including blues, greens, pinks, ambers and yellows as well as dishes, salad bowls and vases. Glasses start at 80F each.

La Chaise Longue

20, Rue des Francs-Bourgeois 75003 (D4)
☎ 01 48 04 36 37
Metro Saint-Paul
Open Mon.-Sat. 11am-7pm,
Sun. 2am-7pm.
8, Rue Princesse 75006 (C4)
☎ 01 43 29 62 39
Metro Mabillon
Closed Sun.
30, Rue Croix-des-Petits-Champs 75001 (C3)
☎ 01 42 96 32 14
Metro Louvre-Rivoli
Closed Sun.

This shop sells a lovely, unpretentious collection, with enamelled crockery in bright colours decorated with exotic flowers or Chinese fish designs. You can also find glasses using contrasting colours and huge plates which can be used as trays. The enamelled plates start at 40F.

Gien

18, Rue de l'Arcade, 75008 (B3)
☎ 01 49 24 07 77
Metro Madeleine
Open Tue.-Sat. 10am-7pm.

This shop sells attractive patterned pieces from the Gien earthenware factory, for everyday use. The contemporary range was created by a team of young designers and features floral patterns and bright fresh colours. You can personalise your plates by adding your initials. Prices start at 395F for a set of dessert plates. Collector's pieces can be ordered by mail from the catalogue.

RUE ROYALE

This is the perfect name for this street, which is full of prestigious stores specialising in tableware (crystal, porcelain and others). From the Place de la Concorde to the Madeleine, the streets are lined with the window displays of Christofle, Ercuis, St-Hilaire, Coquet, Lalique, and Bernardaud (with a tearoom at no. 9). Have a look at Villeroy and Boch, Baccarat, and Saint-Louis too.

Simon

36, Rue Étienne-Marcel, 75002 (C3)
☎ 01 42 33 71 65
Metro Les Halles
Mon.-Sat. 8.30am-6.30pm.

Simon sells white crockery for hotels and English porcelain. The collections of plates, dishes and glasses (nearly 15,000 different items) are displayed very stylishly. Most professional caterers and hotel suppliers will only come to this shop. You can have your silver cutlery restored here (35F per item). It's a mecca for cooks and gourmets.

Jean-Pierre de Castro

17, Rue des Francs-Bourgeois, 75004 (D4)
☎ 01 42 72 04 00
Metro Saint-Paul
Open Mon. 2-7pm, Tue.-Fri. 10.30am-1pm, 2-7pm, Sat. 10am-7pm, Sun. 11am-1pm, 2-7pm.

For all kinds of silverware for every occasion (see p. 62).

Galerie Sentou

18 and 24, Rue du Pont Louis Philippe, 74004 (C4)
☎ 01 42 71 00 01
Metro Saint-Paul
Open Mon.-Fri. 11am-2pm, 3-7pm, Sat. 11am-7pm.

The shop at no. 18 is entirely devoted to tableware. Our favourite range is the *Tsé-Tsé*, by two young women famous for their 'Avril' vase. Don't forget to stop at no. 24 to see the fabrics and curtains by Robert le Héros.

Dehillerin

18, Rue Coquillière, 75001 (C3)
☎ 01 42 36 53 13
Metro Louvre-Rivoli or Étienne Marcel
Open Mon. 8am-12.30pm, 2-6pm,Tue.-Sat. 8am-6pm.

Everything for the kitchen for the professional or amateur (see p. 56).

La Maison Ivre

38, Rue Jacob, 75006 (C4)
☎ 01 42 60 01 85
Metro Saint-Germain-des-Prés
Open Tue.-Sat. 10.30am-7pm.

The crockery here is handcrafted, in the vivid blue, yellow and

green colours of Provence. You'll find unusual patterns and a selection of printed tablecloths with fruit and flower designs, which go well with the natural motifs on the pottery. Decorated plates start at 135F, plain plates from 75F.

Quartz

12, Rue des Quatre-Vents, 75006 (C4)
☎ 01 43 54 03 00
Metro Odéon
Open Mon. 2.30-7pm, Tue.-Sat. 10.30am-7pm.

This is the ultimate glassware shop with artists' original designs alongside the simplest of glasses. There are exclusive signed pieces together with everyday objects, including decanters, plates, vases, candleholders and cheese covers. Choose from dishes and salad bowls in red, green, blue or amber. Classic decanters start at 160F and the square 'Zen' plate costs 290F.

Siècle

24, Rue du Bac, 75007 (B4)
☎ 01 47 03 48 03
Metro Rue du Bac
Open Mon.-Sat. 10.30am-7pm.

Elegant objects of unique and ornate design (see p. 45).

Boutique Paris Musées

Forum des Halles, 1, Rue Pierre Lescot, 75001 (C3)
☎ 01 40 26 56 65
Metro Les Halles
Open Tue.-Sat. 10.30am-7pm, Mon. 2-7pm.

These two shops sell the works of contemporary designers, inspired by Parisian museums or their own imagination. A selection of tableware

for everyday use or for special occasions is available including the Gien 'Majolica' service (60-400F) and the 'Faitoo' series by Philippe Starck (35-500F).

Taïr Mercier

7, Blvd Saint-Germain, 75005 (C4)
☎ 01 43 54 19 97
Metro Maubert-Mutualité
Open Tue.-Fri. 11am-7pm, Sat. 2.30-7pm.

Why not treat yourself to a complete set of Taïr Mercier plastic-coated tablemats and make every meal a party (25-65F). There are exclusive designs for plates at reasonable prices (from 25F), glasses (from 10F), cutlery and even paper serviettes. Some pieces are unique, and handmade plates cost from 120F.

CONTEMPORARY DESIGN

The addresses that we have given here are all well known to French interior designers and stylists. The furniture and smaller items on sale are often signature pieces and sometimes limited editions, though of course prices will reflect this. Modern pieces are not always to everyone's taste, but don't forget today's design may become tomorrow's classic, so see if you can discover the new Philippe Starck.

of the original illustration. Alongside reproductions of master paintings, tapestries and old maps of Paris, you can also find mystery puzzles which have no illustration of the final work. Prices start at 145F for a 100-piece puzzle.

Artistes et Modèles

3, Rue Jacques-Callot, 75006 (C4)
☎ 01 46 33 83 20
Metro Odéon
Open Tues.-Sat. 11am-1pm, 2.30am-7pm.

This is a little shop in the Beaux-Arts neighbourhood. You'll find a reproduction of the chrome and leather armchair (1927) by Mies van der Rohe, and the genuine Thonet seat, which featured in all of Le Corbusier's interiors. There are contemporary designs too, like the Ron Arad bookcase, the Philippe Starck ashtray and his *dadada* stool, plus works by Charlotte Maugirard. Vases by Gaetano Pesce cost from 360F.

Michèle Wilson

116, Rue du Château, 5014 (B5)
☎ 01 43 22 28 73
Metro Pernety

Mon.-Fri. 9am-8pm, Sat. 10am-7pm.

The tradition of hand-crafted wooden puzzles lives on in this shop. Cut by hand, the pieces follow the style and the colours

Astier de Villatte

105, Ave. Daumesnil, 75012 (D4)
☎ 01 43 45 72 72
Metro Bastille or Gare de Lyon
Open Mon.-Fri. 8.30am-6.30pm.

A stylish mix of the modern and the traditional in a collection full of nostalgia, but with a few original touches. Alongside enamelled terracotta from a Parisian workshop there are vases, bowls and crockery. Everything is handmade and plates start at 160F, vases at 540F.

Via

Viaduc des Arts, 29-37 Ave. Daumesnil, 75012 (D4)
☎ 01 46 28 11 11
Metro Gare de Lyon or Bastille
Open Mon.-Fri. 10am-7pm.

This is not just a shop but also a gallery, where you can see the latest trends in the French furnishings industry. There's a thematic exhibition every six weeks, focussing on different subjects. The building itself is also of interest as the shop is located under the arches of an old viaduct.

The whole district is being renovated, the arcades are filling up with boutiques and workshops. The old railway has been replaced with a new terraced garden, part of the *coulée verte* (green trail), which goes almost all the way to the Parc de Vincennes.

Jean-Charles de Castelbajac

6, Pl. Saint-Sulpice, 75006 (C4)
☎ 01 46 33 87 32
Metro Saint-Sulpice
Open Mon.-Sat. 10am-7pm.

Jean-Charles can make a coat from a rug, or a reversible sofa cover which looks good enough to wear. His key words are fun and comfort, featuring natural fabrics, dazzling colours and original details. Cups with wings, lamps disguised as mirrors and rugs with messages on them are some of the very creative things he has on sale.

Axis

Marché Saint-Germain, Saint-Sulpice entrance:
14, rue Lobineau, 75006 (C4)
☎ 01 43 29 66 23
Metro Mabillon
Open Mon.-Sat. 10am-8pm.
13, Rue de Charonne, 75011 (D4)

☎ 01 48 06 79 10
Metro Bastille
Open Tue.-Sat. 11am-7.30pm.

This is a shop absolutely full of humour and creativity, where everyday objects become fun. Crockery, vases, lights and rugs are all given a new look by artists and illustrators.

Miller et Bertaux

17, Rue Ferdinand-Duval, 75004 (C3)
☎ 01 42 78 28 39
Metro Hôtel-de-Ville
Open Mon. 2-7pm,
Tue.-Sat. 11am-1.30pm, 2-7pm.

This shop has items from all over the world, reworked by Miller and Bertaux. You'll find Japanese-inspired flowing clothes and delicate fragrances. It's a unique shop, where everything is chosen to appeal to the senses and emotions.

Xanadou

10, Rue Saint-Sulpice, 75006 (C4)
☎ 01 43 26 73 43
Metro Mabillon or Odéon

Open Tue.-Sat. 11am-1pm, 2-7pm.

Xanadou sells objects designed by architects from all over the world. These are timeless pieces, built to last, including Mackintosh cutlery (1904), the Malevitch teapot (1919) and Joseph Hoffmann glasses. Prices range from 120F for an Enzo Mari paper knife, to 5000F for a crystal bowl by Borek Sipek.

PHILIPPE STARCK

One of the top designers working today, Starck has made quite a name for himself on the international scene, far beyond his native France. His modern and stylish designs for the interiors of the Royalton and Paramount hotels in New York drew much praise. However, if a trip to the Big Apple is not on the cards for the moment, you can always buy a little piece of Starck to take home with you. His famous lemon squeezer reminiscent of a 1950s-style rocket sells at around 400 F, or for a more modest sum you can buy his Dr Skud fly swat bearing the faint imprint of a face, though you may also be able to find these items in some shops at home.

FABRICS AND FURNISHINGS

If you're looking for inspiration, then Paris won't disappoint you. It has many shops and boutiques catering to those wishing to furnish their home in the French style, but it's also a wonderful destination for those looking for new ideas from different lands and cultures. Hand-woven fabrics, furniture and accessories made by local craftsmen, exotic items from India, China, Japan, Mexico and Africa – Paris has them all. You'll have the whole world at your feet (or in your shopping bag).

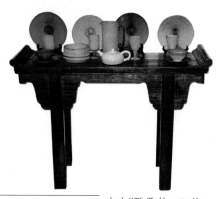

Compagnie Française de l'Orient et de la Chine

260, Blvd Saint-Germain, 75007 (B4)
☎ 01 47 05 92 82
Metro Solférino
Open Mon.-Sat. 10.30am-7pm.
163, 167, Blvd Saint-Germain, 75006 (C4)
☎ 01 45 48 00 18
and 01 45 48 10 31
Metro Saint-Germain-des-Prés
Open Mon.-Sat. 10am-7pm.

Come to these shops for all things Chinese, from ceramics and the furniture of old Peking (at no. 260), to handicrafts (no. 167) and clothes (no. 163). You'll find Cantonese red plates, bowls, flowerpot holders, vases and jars and traditional blue motifs on hand-painted porcelain

bowls (17F). The blue cotton Mao jacket is still a fashion classic (295F) and the smart city version in shantung costs around 1300F.

Liwan

8, Rue Saint-Sulpice, 75006 (C4)
☎ 01 43 26 07 40
Metro Saint-Sulpice

Open Mon. 2-7pm, Tue.-Sat. 10.30am-7pm.

This is the place to discover the work of the Lebanese designer Lina Audi, with her stylised versions of Lebanese and Mediterranean craftsmanship. There's a very pretty collection of curtains, household linen, tablecloths, bedspreads and cotton bath towels. Try the soft, lovely Aleppo soap for 50F.

Caravane

6, Rue Pavée, 75004 (D4)
☎ 01 44 61 04 20
Metro Saint-Paul
Open Tue.-Sat. 11am-7pm.

For fabrics, rugs, wall-hangings and goods from Asia or Africa (see p. 63).

Le Jardin Moghol

53, Rue Vieille-du-Temple, 75004 (D4)
☎ 01 48 87 41 32
Metro Saint-Paul
Open Tue.-Sat. 10am-7pm.

Imagine yourself travelling on the Indian sub-continent in the time of the Maharajahs, with these 15th-and 16th-century woven cotton and silk designs for bed and cushion covers and tablecloths. You'll find clothes, furniture and smaller items in a rainbow of colours. There are also beautiful curtains made with printed panels and silk and wool wraps (from 490F).

L'Atelier 74

74, Rue de la Verrerie, 75004 (C3)
Metro Hôtel de Ville.

Paris is a European capital with a truly cosmopolitan feel. There are many shops that specialise in crafts, clothes and jewellery from all around the world. Parisians love a touch of the exotic. At Atelier 74, international craftsmen are able to exhibit their work for a few weeks at a time. African jewellery, Native American fabrics, beads and leatherware are displayed alongside sculptures, precious objects and trinkets. The Atelier is an interesting place full of the inspiration and variety that the international artists bring with them.

Galerie Bamyan

24, Rue Saint-Louis-en-l'Île, 75004 (C4)
☎ 01 46 33 69 66
Metro Pont Marie
Open Tue.-Sat. 11.30am-8pm, Sun. 2-8pm.

A shop full of the kind of treasures acquired by an anthropologist during his travels. It includes handicrafts from central Asia, Indian bridal jewellery and lovely examples of traditional furniture adapted to modern tastes. Coffee tables cost from 700 to 2500F.

Le Monde Sauvage

101, Rue Saint-Denis, 75001 (C3)
☎ 01 40 26 28 81
Metro Étienne Marcel
Open Mon. 1.30-7.30pm, Tue.-Sat. 10.30am-7.30pm.

This store comes as a surprise in a street full of clothes boutiques and sex-shops. You'll find antiques and copies of colonial furniture, along with goods from Asia and Central Europe. Wood, wrought iron, glass, wickerwork and fabrics are all for sale. A small Indian wooden table costs 700F and a wrought-iron candleholder with 5 candles will set you back 100F.

La Ville de Mogador

16, Rue du Vieux-Colombier, 75006 (B4)
☎ 01 45 48 04 48
Metro Saint-Sulpice
Open Tue.-Sat. 10am-2pm, 3-7pm.

This place has the atmosphere of an oriental bazaar, with rugs, pottery, Moroccan copper lanterns and hand-painted ceramic plates. The familiar tea-glasses that everyone loves cost 25F and earthenware cooking pots are from 250 to 600F.

Galerie Urubamba

4, Rue de la Bûcherie, 75005 (C4)
☎ 01 43 54 08 24
Metro Maubert-Mutualité
Open Tue.-Sat. 2-7.30pm.

Named after the sacred valley of the Incas, this is the place to discover the crafts and traditions of tribes from the three Americas. It sells Alpaca ponchos, embroidered blouses, Peruvian fabrics, ceramics and wickerwork. You can buy colourful beads to make your own jewellery and books, cassettes and CDs. Try a pair of authentic Indian moccasins at 300F.

HOUSEHOLD LINEN

Do you feel like spoiling yourself with romantic lace-edged sheets, a special occasion tablecloth embroidered with a pretty floral pattern, a soft dressing gown to keep you warm during the cold winter months, or luxurious towels in all sizes and colours? Then Paris is the place for you, and these are our suggestions for some of the best shops to try.

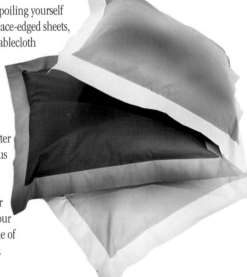

Atout Blanc

20, Rue de Rivoli, 75004 (D4)
☎ **01 48 04 98 50**
Metro Saint-Paul
Open Mon. 3-7pm, Tue.-Fri. 11am-7pm, Sat. 10.30am-1.30pm, 2-7pm.

ATOUT BLANC
20, rue de Rivoli - 75004 Paris
Tél. 48 04 98 50

Despite the name (to all white) you'll find bath towels in more than 20 colours from 59F, superb dressing gowns from 299F, a wide range of quilt covers of all sizes, and tartan rugs from 99F.

Matin Bleu

92, Rue de Rennes, 75006 (B4)
☎ **01 42 22 94 40**
Metro Saint-Sulpice
Open Mon.-Sat. 9am-7pm.

This store has four different lines for different lifestyles: 'natural', 'modern', 'exotic' and 'romantic', so choose the one to suit your mood. There are Italian brands like Jalla and Bassetti, and a 'Matin Bleu'

range at reasonable prices, for the bedroom and dining room. Sheets for a double bed cost from 290F each.

Blanc Cassé

101, Rue du Bac, 75007 (B4)
☎ **01 45 48 87 88**
Metro Sévres-Babylone
Open Mon. noon-7pm, Tue.-Sat. 10am-7pm.

There are bath towels from 60F, dressing gowns for 220F, linen and cotton sheets for 460F. The seconds are unwrapped, but sold at unbeatable prices. This is a real bargain store.

Textures

55, Rue des Saints Pères, 75006 (B4)
☎ **01 45 48 90 88**
Metro Saint-Germain-des-Prés
Open Mon. 2.30-6.30pm, Tue.-Sat. 10am-6.30pm.

Textures is worth a visit for the printed, dyed and embroidered Designers' Guild fabrics. Multi-coloured bath sheets for 265F, bedding for babies, sheets for children and adults from 190F. Beautiful soft furnishing fabrics and even sofas.

WHAT MAKES A GOOD TOWEL?

The ideal material is Egyptian cotton, or a cotton with long fibres. The 'loop' in towelling was invented in the late 19th century. The more threads per square centimetre, the more loops there are, and the greater the quality of the towelling. In other words, heavy equals luxurious as long as the fabric doesn't become too soft. If towelling is shaved on one side, it changes in appearance and is called velvet. You may find you need to wash new towels before using them, to soften them and make them fully absorbant.

La Paresse en Douce

97, Rue du Bac, 75007 (B4)
☎ 01 42 22 64 10
Metro Rue du Bac
Open Tue.-Sat. 11am-7pm,
Mon. 2-7pm.

Depending on the season, buy cuddly flannelette for winter, or silk and cotton for summer. Everything is soft and luxurious—slippers and pyjamas, soft dressing gowns and cushions, cool sheets and cashmere rugs, tablecloths and tablemats. Embroidered towels cost from 120F and cushions cost from 240F.

Porthault

18, Ave. Montaigne, 75008 (A3)
☎ 01 47 20 75 25
Metro Alma-Marceau or Franklin D. Roosevelt
Open Mon. 9.30am-1pm, 2-6.30pm, Tue.-Fri. 9.30am-6.30pm, Sat. 9.30am-1pm, 2-6pm.

An appropriately luxurious shop for a luxurious district – organdie, linen, silk and satin embroidered with leaves and flowers. The sheets, tablecloths, towels and robes are deliciously romantic, with lots of lace and panels. The 'Studio' line is reasonably priced at 180F for tablemats and 300F for an embroidered towel.

Laurence Roque

69, Rue Saint-Martin, 75004 (C3)
☎ 01 42 72 22 12
Metro Châtelet
Open Tue.-Sat. 10.30am-6.30pm, Mon. 1.30-6.30pm.
Closed Sun.

This charming shop specialises in bathroom and table linen, with various styles of embroidery and tapestry. Embroided items cost from 50 to 800F. Sewing enthusiasts will find patterns, threads and fabrics for their favourite hobby here. Whilst the lazy, or less nimble-fingered can buy pre-embroidered articles, like bibs (about 60F each), or laundry bags. Once you've finished your masterpiece, you can also have it framed here. Mail order service available.

Maison de Vacances

63, 64, Galerie de Montpensier, 75001 (C3)
☎ 01 47 03 99 74
Metro Palais-Royal-Musée du Louvre
Open Mon. 1-7pm,
Tue.-Sat. 11am-7pm (see p. 39).

BARGAIN HUNTING

Paris has some great shops where you can buy last season's collections. The clothes may not be 'hot off the catwalk', but there are some real bargains to be had. Here are some of the places you should try.

FABRIC

Les Deux Portes

30, Blvd Henri-IV, 75011 (D4)
☎ 01 42 71 13 02
Metro Bastille
Open Tue.-Sat. 10am-6.30pm.

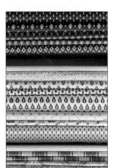

This shop has a selection of fabrics at low prices, including the popular 'Deux Portes' line. There is often a discount of 20% on quality collections and year-round reductions on other fabrics. There is also some choice of silks for furnishings.

Mendès

5, Rue d'Uzès, 75002 (C3)
☎ 01 42 36 02 39
Metro Bonne Nouvelle
Open Mon.-Sat. 10am-6pm

Fabrics made for Yves Saint Laurent and Christian Lacroix supplied directly from the factory. You'll have to wait six months after the fashion shows, but you'll pay up to 50% less, which makes it well worth the wait.

CLOTHES

Le Mouton à Cinq Pattes

8, 10, 18, 48, Rue Saint-Placide, 75006 (B4)
☎ 01 45 48 86 26
Metro Sèvres-Babylone
Open Mon.-Sat. 10am-7pm.
15, Rue Vieille-du-Temple, 75004 (C3)
☎ 01 42 71 86 30
Metro Hôtel-de-Ville
Open Mon.-Fri. 10.30am-7.30pm (closed 2-3pm), Sat. 10.30am-8pm.

A well-known Parisian address, this shop is a classic of its kind, with top quality ready-to-wear clothes from manufacturers all over Europe. The collections arrive here two or three weeks after they've been delivered to the fashion boutiques and are up-to-date, but not over the top. Blazers cost from 299-800F. There are clothes for women, men and children, the latter in the Annexe at no. 48.

L'Annexe des Créateurs

19, Rue Godot de Mauroy, 75009 (B3)
☎ 01 42 65 46 40
Metro Madeleine
Open Mon.-Sat. 10.30am-7pm.

You can enjoy 40-70% reductions all year round on designer and couturier collections. Last season's styles, including designer business suits and cocktail dresses are available together with wonderful accessories. There's a menswear department and a bridal collection. From 390F for a skirt and 990F for a suit.

Chercheminippes

109, 110, 111, Rue du Cherche-Midi, 75006 (B4)
☎ 01 42 22 45 23
Metro Duroc
Open Mon.-Sat. 10.30am-6pm (consignment), 7pm (sales).

FEET STREET

Rue Meslay (métro Strasbourg-Saint-Denis) has more shoe shops than anywhere else in Paris, with retailers, manufacturers and wholesalers located side by side. You'll find one of the best shops at no. 63:

Mart-ine,
63, Rue Meslay, 75003,
☎ 01 42 71 35 09
Open Mon.-Sat. 9am-7pm.
A great place to buy the most fashionable shoes, up-to-the-minute styles for 20-30% less than elsewhere. Doc Martens (from 480F), Timberland, Converse and Caterpillars (to be super cool the French just call these les 'cat') are just some of the big labels.

This is a secondhand shop. The clothes you'll find here are no more than a year old. Women's fashions are at no. 109 (Kenzo, Klein etc), new clothes and haute-couture are at no. 111 (Chanel, Hermès etc) and at no. 110 are men's and children's clothes. Irié jackets for 580F, Aridza Bross T-shirts for 60F, everything is half-price – it's a great find.

Tati

2-42, Blvd Rochechouart, 75018 (C2)
☎ 01 55 29 50 00
Metro Barbès-Rochechouart
Open Mon. 10am-7pm, Tue.-Fri. 9.30am-7pm, Sat. 9.15am-7pm.

Everybody knows about the Tati stores. Eastern Europeans come to do their shopping here. Everyone is keen to see the new goods, even if they don't admit it. The Tati line

'La Rue est à Nous' ('The street belongs to us') is young and trendy, with jumpers from 79F. There's also a children's range called 'L'Avenir est à Nous' ('The future belongs to us'). English-speaking visitors can derive much amusement from the store's name of course, so make sure you at least come away with a Tati carrier bag.

Guerrisold

29-31, Ave. de Clichy, 75017 (B2)
☎ 01 53 42 31 32
Metro Place de Clichy
Open Mon.-Sat. 10am-7.30pm
17a, Blvd Rochechouart, 75018 (C2)
☎ 01 45 26 38 92

Metro Barbès
Open Mon.-Sat. 9am-7.30pm.

At this shop you'll find a huge selection of new and old clothes at unbeatably low prices. It's a good place for some serious browsing. No two items are the same, whatever the size. The 'Delta' line is young and trendy, with shirts from 19-69F. Silk shirts start at 50F and suits cost from 50-120F.

COMPUTERS

Surcouf

139, Ave. Daumesnil, 75012 (D4)
☎ 01 53 33 20 00
Metro Gare de Lyon
Open Tue.-Sat. 9.30am-7pm.

RUE D'ALÉSIA: READY-TO-WEAR BARGAINS

A few stores along a section of the Rue d'Alésia (B5-métro Alésia) have specialised in ready-to-wear designer seconds for the last 15 years.

■ **Cacharel Stock**, at no. 114 ☎ 01 45 42 53 04, has a selection of men's, women's and children's clothes (a wide range of shirts from 220F).

■ **Dorotennis**, at no. 74, has chic sportswear, coordinates and swimwear (50-169F).

■ **Régina Rubens**, 88, Rue d'Alésia, 75014, ☎ 01 40 44 90 05.

■ **Daniel Hechter** (Stock 2), at no. 92, ☎ 01 45 41 65 57, has last season's collections, clothes and accessories for men, women and children.

■ The **Évolutif** shop at no. 139, ☎ 01 45 45 44 83 has a wide range of men's clothes (Cerruti suits from 1,800F, Kenzo pullovers 700F).

This is France's largest computer store, with 300 demonstrators, 250 stands and a vast exhibition area. They've got every imaginable item for your computing needs (PCs, printers, discs and books). There's a secondhand store, as well as a computer flea market where you can sometimes find real bargains.

A GOURMET'S PARADISE

A bit of a cliché perhaps, but since France is famed for being a foodie paradise, it naturally follows that more than a little of this will rub off on its capital. There is certainly nothing quite like the range of immaculately prepared dishes displayed in the windows of the *traiteurs*, nor the cakes in the *patisseries*. It's best not to visit Paris whilst on a diet.

Mariage Frères

30, Rue du Bourg-Tibourg, 75004 (C3)
☎ 01 42 72 28 11
Metro Hôtel-de-Ville
Open every day 10.30am-7.30pm, tearoom open noon-7pm.

This is a wonderful store with hundreds of tins of tea piled high on dark wooden shelves. The sales staff are experts and will always take the time to guide you in your choice. They also have a range of teapots and teacups, adapted from traditional Chinese

and Japanese designs. Try the chocolate or green-tea cake in the tearoom.

Jadis et gourmande

88, Blvd. du Port-Royal, 75005 (C5)
☎ 01 43 26 17 75
Metro Port-Royal
Open Tue.-Sat. 9.30am-7pm, Mon. 1-7pm.

Chocolate in all shapes and sizes is displayed on wooden shelves in this cosy shop. The specialities include twists of plain or milk chocolate with dried fruit, orange flavoured chocolate in the shape of a crown and chocolate from various countries (with information about each one). Send a chocolate birthday postcard (42F) complete with envelope to keep the greeting intact.

Debauve et Gallais

30, Rue des Saints-Pères, 75006 (B4)
☎ 01 45 48 54 67
Metro Saint-Germain-des-Prés
33, Rue Vivienne, 75002
☎ 01 40 39 05 50
Metro Bourse
Open Mon.-Sat. 9am-7pm.

Wooden counters with chocolates lined up like little soldiers, just waiting to be eaten. This shop once supplied goods to Louis XVIII and Charles X. It was Debauve who invented sugar-free, vanilla and orange chocolate – items still sold today, for 95F per box. The latest creation is aptly named 'The Incredible One' (*l'Incroyable*) and is a delicious nougat concoction.

L'Herboristerie du Palais-Royal

11, Rue des Petits-Champs, 75001 (C3)
☎ 01 42 97 54 68
Metro Palais-Royal-Musée du Louvre
Open Mon.-Fri. 9.30am-7pm, Sat. 10.30am-6.30pm.

Natural wood and wickerwork create a lovely backdrop for the hundreds of medicinal and aromatic plants in this shop. There are cosmetics made from plant extracts plus essential oils for the hair, face and body and rose and jasmine fragrances to perfume the bath or the home. A bottle of wheatgerm oil costs 78F.

Faguais

30, Rue de La Trémoille, 75008 (A3)
☎ 01 47 20 80 91
Metro George-V
Open Mon.-Sat. 9.15am-7pm.

This old-fashioned shop, where the cash register is still behind a glass partition, has been importing the best Arabica coffee since 1912 – Ethiopian Mocha, Salvadorian Pacarama, Jamaican Blue Mountain. The coffee is roasted to order and the store also sells luxury groceries, including superb teas and delicious honeys.

Verlet

256, Rue Saint-Honoré, 75001 (C3)
☎ 01 42 60 67 39
Metro Palais-Royal-Musée du Louvre
Open Tue.-Sat. 9am-7pm (winter), Mon.-Fri. 9am-7pm (May-Oct.), tearoom open 9am-6pm.

At Verlet coffee is an art form, like poetry or music. They create their own blends that change with the seasons—milder in summer, stronger in autumn. You can taste freshly roasted coffee on the spot—Arabica from Jamaica, Hawaii and Columbia, and over 20 Verlet varieties. Teas, dried and candied fruits and ice-creams are also available.

Olsen Bornholm

8, Rue du Commandant Rivière, 75008 (A3)
☎ 01 45 61 22 64
Metro St-Philippe-du-Roule.
Open Mon.-Sat. noon-3pm, 7-11pm.

This shop imports goods direct from the Baltic and is a favourite spot of Scandinavians living in the city. Smoked salmon and

eels make the journey to Paris. Don't miss the superb marzipan. If you can't hold out there are a few tables in the shop itself at which you can sample the goodies immediately.

PARISIAN MARKETS

Parisian markets date back to the Middle Ages, but many of them are still the lifeblood of the capital. Our selection includes some of the most attractive and unusual markets. You'll enjoy both the atmosphere and the wonderful produce.

FOOD

Tang Frères
48, Ave d'Ivry, 75013 (D5)
Metro Porte d'Ivry
Open every day 9am-7.30pm. Closed Mon.

This incredible Asian supermarket is usually very crowded. You'll find Chinese cabbage, kumquats, Basmati rice, sticky rice, dim sum (20F per dozen), meat, fish, bonsai, crockery, Chinese beer, and a selection of ready-made dishes. There's colour, atmosphere and unbeatable prices. For the price of a metro ticket, spend a Sunday afternoon in Asia whilst the rest of Paris is closed.

Belleville market
On the central section dividing the Blvd de Belleville, 75020 (E3)
Metro Belleville
Open Tue. & Fri. 7am-1.30pm.

People come here from all over Paris to find plantains, yams and exotic fruits. Many West Indian, African and Asian restaurants stock up here. There's a wide selection of fresh herbs and spices. Wend your way among the colourful stalls and enjoy the exotic atmosphere and tempting aromas.

Raspail organic market
Blvd Raspail, between Rue du Cherche-Midi and Rue de Rennes, 75006 (B4)
Metro Sèvres-Babylone or Rennes
Open Sun. morning.

Health conscious Parisians frequent this pretty market with its organically grown produce. The prices are on the high side,

but you will find all kinds of vegetables, such as squash, pumpkin and Chinese cabbage. There are also charcuterie stalls and regional products.

Mouffetard market
Rue Mouffetard, as far as the Place de la Contrescarpe, 75005 (C4-5)
Metro Censier-Daubenton
Open Tue.-Sat. 9am-1pm, 4-9.30pm, Sun. morning.

Parisians call this market 'La Mouff'. It's famous for its fruit, vegetables and charcuterie. With its colourful stalls, old church and accordionist, it looks like a film set of the Paris

you've always imagined (with the addition of rather a lot of tourists). It's a good place for a Sunday-morning outing.

Aligre market

Rue d'Aligre, 75012 (D4)
Metro Ledru-Rollin
Open every day 8am-1pm,
3-30-7.30pm, Sun. 8am-
1pm. Closed Mon.

Although it's not far from the
trendy Bastille district, the Place
d'Aligre is still an authentic
Parisian market, mostly run by
North African stallholders. The
Beauveau market is in a beautiful
19th-century building, worth a visit
for its paving stones and fountain.
There are excellent charcuterie
and cheese delicatessens and
several secondhand clothes stalls.
This is Paris's cheapest and
liveliest market.

FABRIC

Marché Saint-Pierre

2, Rue Charles-Nodier,
75018 (C2)
☎ 01 46 06 92 25
Metro Anvers
Open Tue.-Sat. 9.15am-
6.30pm, Mon. 1-6.30pm.

This big fabric store is a paradise
for dressmakers and home
decoration enthusiasts. The silk

THE BIRD/FLOWER MARKET (MARCHÉ AUX OISEAUX/AUX FLEURS)

Place Louis-Lépine,
75004 (C4)
Metro Cité
Open Mon.-Sat. 8am-
7.30pm

A stone's throw from
the Palais de Justice,
the Ile de la Cité becomes a
blaze of colour with primroses,
geraniums, rhododendrons
and hydrangeas, plus a huge
selection of bonsai. The bird
market takes over on Sundays
from 8am to 7.30pm. The air is
full of the trill of canaries,
mynabirds, budgerigars and
rare birds. On the Quai de la
Mégisserie, across the river,
there are pet shops where you
can buy fish from all over the
world (open Sun.).

shop on the second floor is the best
in Paris. Furnishing fabrics are on
the third floor and household linen
on the fourth. A couple of metres of
woollen cloth start at about 20F.

The **Reine** store just across
the street specialises in soft
furnishing fabrics. The surrounding streets are lined with fabric
retail outlets, and you'll find a
larger selection of fabrics in this
area than anywhere else in the
entire country.

BOOKS AND STAMPS

Book market (Marché aux livres)

Rue Brancion, 75015 (A5)
Metro Porte de Vanves
Open Sat. & Sun. 9.30am-6pm.

Every weekend the Georges
Brassens park becomes a meeting
place for impoverished intellectuals
and booklovers. Secondhand books
for 10F, comic strips and vintage
editions of Tintin or rare books can
be found in this covered market,
which is a bookworm's delight.

Stamp market (Marché aux timbres)

On the corner of Ave. Marigny
and Ave. Gabriel, 75008 (A3)
Metro Franklin D. Roosevelt
Open Thur. Sat. Sun. &
holidays 10am-sunset.

This open-air Parisian institution
is the favourite haunt of stamp
and telephone card collectors.
You may well find the missing
piece to complete your collection,
but you have to be prepared to
pay for it. There is also a large
selection of old postcards,
classified according to theme
or region. You can get an idea
of what Paris looked like at the
turn of the century.

FLEA MARKETS AND ANTIQUES

With more than 4,000 antique or secondhand dealers and the largest auction room in the country, Paris and the surrounding area is the heart of France's national art market. You can buy or sell everything from teddy bears to sedan chairs. Put your credit cards away and get ready to bargain!

People come from all over to find a specific object or simply browse. It's a favourite Sunday outing for Parisians all year round, and it's especially popular with tourists during the summer months. Don't expect to get great bargains, but you'll find all kinds of things in the 2,000 open or covered stalls. The salespeople know their stuff, and if you find the prices high, it's due to the fact that there are customers willing to pay that much. However, you can always try to negotiate the price–a discount of 10% on the asking price is quite common. If you persist you might get a reduction of 25 or 30%. All the stallholders work with carriers who can arrange delivery throughout the world. Check the prices, though, as delivery will obviously push the price up.

Hôtel Drouot

9, Rue Drouot, 75009 (C3)
☎ 01 48 00 20 20
Metro Richelieu-Drouot
Lots are displayed the day before the sale (11am-6pm) and the morning of the sale (11am-noon). Sales 2-6pm.

You can save a lot of money by buying at an auction rather than from an antique dealer. Auction sales are often where the dealers will have bought the pieces in the first place, but then add a percentage for themselves. All auction sales are advertised in *La Gazette de l'hôtel Drouot* (13.50F from news stands). The lots can be viewed prior to the sale, so take your time and look at each piece carefully. You're free to pick up objects you're interested in. If you're not present on the day of the

auction, you can leave a bid with the auctioneer. The item will be yours if your price is not outbid. There are no auctions in Paris at weekends, but you could try Versailles or Saint-Germain. All the relevant information is in *La Gazette*.

Saint-Ouen flea market (Marché aux Puces de St-Ouen)

Rue des Rosiers, St Ouen, 75018
Metro Porte de Clignancourt (C1)
Open Sat.-Mon. 8am-6pm.

Saint-Ouen consists of several separate specialist markets, and is the oldest and the most crowded of the Parisian flea markets.

Paul Bert market
Rue Paul Bert

This may be the last flea market where you can still find authentic secondhand stalls, selling ironware, garden furniture, objects from the 1950s and 1960s, glassware and earthenware.

Biron market
Rue des Rosiers

This market is divided into two. There's a covered section which specialises in good quality rustic and regional furniture, and there's an open-air section which is much more flashy, with lots of crystal and period furniture with gilded bronzes. A few stalls deal in Art Nouveau and Art Deco pieces, and you'll also find fans and glassware. There's a transport company at the entrance to the market for your heavier purchases.

Rosiers market
Rue Paul Bert

This is the place for decorative glass and ceramic objects from the turn of the century, with plenty of Lalique, Gallé and Decorchemont. Everything is beautiful but expensive.

Serpette market
Rue des Rosiers

This market opened recently with plenty of Art Deco and Art Nouveau objects, paintings and furniture (although not always restored in the best of taste). Prices can be rather high.

Jules Vallès market
Rue Jules-Vallès

A great place for old postcards, old toys, garden furniture and lots of bric-a-brac. It's good for turn of the century *objects d'arts*.

Vernaison market
Ave. Michelet

This is a maze of a market. Good for rugs, regional earthenware, and ornaments. There's a fun stall that sells old spectacles. Visit the Chez Louisette café.

Malassis market
Rue des Rosiers

The stalls in this new, light and airy market tell you which periods are back in vogue, which could be anything from Art Deco, 1950s or Napoleon III. There are not many large items of furniture, mostly small china or ornaments, paintings and sculptures. Prices are on the high side.

Dauphine market
Rue des Rosiers

This market is on two floors and sells engravings, paintings, ornaments, beautiful furniture from the 18th century to the 1950s, earthenware, porcelain, old books and papers.

Montreuil flea market
Ave. du Professeur-André-Lemierre, 75020 (F4)
Metro Porte de Montreuil
Open Sun. & Mon. 8am-6pm.

You'll find some general second-hand goods here but of no great

interest, some great 1960s and 1970s clothes. Have fun dressing up for next to nothing.

Vanves flea market
Ave. Georges-Lafenestre, 75014 (B6)
Metro Porte de Vanves
Open Sat. & Sun. 7am-7.30pm.

These are good general stalls

selling knick-knacks, curios, books, earthenware, paintings and household furniture from the late 1800s to the present day. This market is considerably cheaper than Saint-Ouen (antique dealers themselves stock up here). It's the perfect place for unearthing an unusual treasure. Highly recommended.

Nightlife

Paris is no more dangerous at night than any other city, but certain areas are best avoided after 1am. These include Stalingrad, Barbès and Les Halles, but on the whole you'll have little to fear. The last metro isn't always the best place to try and make friends, but it's reasonably safe. Here are a few ideas and suggestions on how to make your evenings out go smoothly.

GETTING AROUND AT NIGHT

Metro: All the métro lines operate from 5.30am until about 12.30am, when the last train leaves the station.

Bus: The following buses run until 12.30am:
21, 26, 27, 31, 38, 52, 62, 63, 72, 74, 80, 85, 91, 92, 95.
Timetables are displayed at bus stops; buses usually come every 15-30 minutes. Other bus services stop between 8.30- 9pm.

The RATP (Parisian transport authority) has started up a *Noctambus* service, linking Paris and the suburbs. Buses run from 1am-5.30am. The price of a ride, regardless of the destination, with or without transfers is 30F Only the west of Paris is not covered by these night routes.

Taxi: About 2,000 of the 15,500 or so taxi drivers work at night. It's best to phone for a taxi, but you can often get one from a taxi rank or stop one in the street. The pick-up fee (at a rank) is 13F. From 7pm-7am, and on Sundays and national holidays, tariff B is in operation (5.45F per km/0.62 miles). Otherwise during the day (7am-7pm) and within the *Periphérique* (Paris ring road) the A tariff is in operation (3.45F per km/0.62 miles). Luggage is charged at 6F per piece. if you are picked up at a main-line station there is also an additional charge of 5F.

If you ask a taxi driver to wait for you, the charge is around 130F per hour. If you want to do a tour of Paris by night to see the lights, it will cost you about 75F for 30 minutes.

Limousine: So you want to play the VIP (even if it means emptying your piggy-bank)? Contact International Limousines, 182, Blvd Péreire, 75017, ☎ 01 53 81 14 00. From 8pm-12am, you'll have a chauffeur and a Mercedes 300 SEL (four-door) or a Silverstar six-door for 422F per hour. On Sundays, you'll have to pay a weekend supplement of 110F: peanuts!

WHAT'S ON?

Most daily papers, such as *le Figaro, le Monde* and *Libération,* have fairly complete entertainment pages. However, the Bible for entertainment is still *Pariscope* (3F) or

l'Officiel des Spectacles (2F), both of which come out every Wednesday. This is also the day new movies come out and the programmes change.

WHAT TIME DO PEOPLE GO OUT?

The French generally go out for dinner to a restaurant from 8pm (some restaurants have two sittings and serve meals until quite late). They go to cafés between 6 and 8pm, to the Opera around 7.30pm, to the theatre at 8.30pm and 9pm. Concerts ususally start at 8.30pm, but nightclubs don't get going before 11 or 11.30pm.

WHAT SHOULD YOU WEAR?

If you're going to eat in a top-notch restaurant, you should wear a jacket and tie, or a suit. People rarely dress up for the opera or theatre nowadays, except on opening nights. If you go clubbing, wear whatever's in fashion (with or without tie, it varies). In trendy bars, pubs or cafés, dress as you like. Sneakers or trainers, however, don't always go down well, so be warned!

FOR NIGHT OWLS

If you have an irresistible urge to see a movie at midnight, check out the programs of the UGC cinemas on the Champs-Élysées, or the Gaumont cinemas in Montparnasse and at the Étoile, and at the Publicis Élysées.

Feeling peckish? The Ancienne Comédie bakery (10, Rue de l'Ancienne-Comédie, 75006, ☎ 01 43 26 89 72) is open 24 hours a day.

Desperate to hear some jazz? Champs Disques (84, Ave des Champs-Élysées, 75008) is open Monday to Saturday, 9am to midnight; Sunday, noon to 8pm. The Virgin Megastore (52, Ave des Champs-Élysées ☎ 01 49 53 50 00) is open Monday to Saturday 10am to midnight, Sunday and holidays noon to midnight.

KEEPING UP WITH THE NEWS

The following news stands are open non-stop: 33 and 60, Champs-Élysées; Place de l'Etoile; and16, Blvd de la Madeleine.

The Prisunic at 26, Rue d'Astorg, ☎ 01 42 65 44 16, is open until midnight; the **Drugstores Publicis** at 133, Ave des Champs-Élysées ☎ 01 44 43 79 00, and 1, Ave Matignon ☎ 01 43 59 38 70 are open every day 9am-2am.

If you need some bedtime reading, why not head for the **Virgin Megastore** or **Mots à la Bouche**, 6, Rue Sainte-Croix-de-la-Bretonnerie, ☎ 01 42 78 88 30 (open till 11pm, Mon. to Sat., to 8pm on Sun.); the **l'Écume des Pages**, 174, Blvd Saint-Germain, 75006, ☎ 01 45 48 54 48, open till midnight (closed Sun.); **La Hune,** 170, Blvd Saint-Germain, 75006, ☎ 01 45 48 35 85, open till 11.45pm (closed Sun.); or the **Marché Saint-André,** 40, Rue Saint-André-des-Arts, 75006, ☎ 01 43 26 16 03, also open till midnight.

NIGHTLIFE

Even if you only have a couple of days to spend in Paris, remember that this city has it all. If you're looking for a concert or an opera, a friendly pavement café or a trendy basement bar, a lively jazz club or a famous nightclub, a ballet or a cabaret, you won't be disappointed. Here are a few suggestions on how to spend your 48 hours in one of the most exciting capitals in Europe.

Paris by night

One of the most romantic ways to see the lights of Paris is from the water, see page 119. Alternatively you can take to the road and take a taxi or even a limousine ride, but see p. 116 first. Our proposed route follows the Seine from the Maison de la Radio to Bercy. You'll pass the Trocadéro, opposite the Eiffel Tower, the Place de la Concorde, and continue alongside the Tuileries Gardens. You'll see the Musée d'Orsay on the opposite bank and the newly renovated dome of the Institute of France on the left bank, as long as you don't take the tunnel. A little further along you'll see Perrault's Colonnade at the Louvre museum. La Samaritaine department store is in a wonderful Art Deco building overlooking the Seine and the Pont Neuf, which is also illuminated at night. As you arrive at the Île de la Cité you'll see the façade of the Conciergerie, followed by the Place du Châtelet, with the Palmier fountain between the two theatres. The Tribunal de Commerce has an illuminated dome, and the imposing Notre-Dame Cathedral is magnificent at night. The brightly lit Place de l'Hôtel de Ville is next, after which you reach the Marais, with its marvellous old buildings and beautiful façades. If you look across to the opposite bank you'll see the Île Saint Louis and its wonderful 17th-century mansions. Drive under the Austerlitz bridge and along the river through the futurist buildings of the Bercy district. Your journey will end at the Ministry of Finances. To view Paris from the river itself, try one of the following river trips.

Lamoureux concerts on Sunday at 5.45pm. Performances run from 20 September to 20 June. Make a telephone reservation, Mon.-Fri. 10am-6pm, two weeks in advance, or buy your tickets direct from the box office (Mon.-Sat. 11am-6pm) the day of the concert. You can also order tickets by mail with a stamped, self-addressed envelope up to two months ahead. Ticket prices range from 65-190F

By Boat

Bateaux Parisiens

☎ 01 44 11 33 55, Port de la Bourdonnais (in front of the Eiffel Tower). Free parking for three hours, access via Quai Branly opposite Avenue de la Bourdonnais. The trip lasts an hour, with departures every 30 minutes from 10am-10pm (except at 7.30pm). It costs 50F per person, 25F for the under 12s. The dinner cruise costs 560F, 8-11pm with classical music (orchestra and singer). The boat travels from Bercy to the Statue of Liberty. The dress code is smart.

By Yacht

The *Don Juan*

This is a 1930s boat with mahogany and teak fittings, a black marble fireplace in the large lounge and comfortable armchairs. This is a cruise for foodlovers, with a menu dreamed up by Gérard Besson. Lobster salads, foie gras and lots more. It costs 790F per person with a half-bottle of wine. The boat leaves at 9pm and returns around 11pm.

Concerts

Salle Pleyel

252, Rue du Faubourg Saint-Honoré, 75008 (A2)
☎ 01 45 61 53 00
Metro Ternes.

The philharmonic orchestra of Radio France plays every Friday at 8pm. Pasdeloup concerts are on Saturday at 5.30pm and

Cité de la Musique

221, Ave. Jean-Jaurès, 75019 (E2)
Metro Pantin
☎ 01 44 84 44 84.

The architect Christian de Portzamparc designed this building with a concert hall, museum amphitheatre and area for free concerts. Book by post at least 3 weeks ahead, by phone, or at the box office (open every day, from noon-6pm, Sun. 10am-6pm).

You can sometimes buy tickets at the box office 30 minutes before a concert. The repertoire includes classical and baroque music, jazz, rock, traditional French songs and contemporary performances.

Opera

Opéra Garnier

Pl. de l'Opéra, 75009 (C3)
Metro Opéra
☎ 01 40 01 17 89

Opéra Bastille

120, Rue de Lyon, 75012 (D4)
Metro Bastille
☎ 08 36 69 78 68

You can buy tickets at the opera itself or via an agency, but do so well in advance. The opulence of the Opéra Garnier, both inside and out, is staggering. Worth a visit for the building alone, but tickets are from 60-590F.

Péniche Opéra

Opposite 200, Quai de Jemmapes, 75010 (D2)
Metro Jaurès
☎ **01 42 45 18 20 (bookings)**
☎ **01 53 38 49 40 (info)**

This renovated barge near the Hôtel du Nord has daily performances at 9pm, Sundays at 5pm. The productions and shows are taken from classical and contemporary repertoires. Tickets from 60-250F.

Jazz

La Villa

29, Rue Jacob, 75006 (C4)
Metro Saint-Germain-des-Prés.
☎ **01 43 26 60 00**
Concerts every day at 10.30pm
Closed Sun. and Aug.

In the basement of a 4-star hotel with modern decor by Marie-Christine Dorner, this club has a new programme every week. Listen to quartets and quintets, American and European artists, a wide range of genres and some well-known names, including Ceccarelli, Roney, Van Freeman, Kurt Elling. New talents are welcome as well. Admission is 120F including one drink, 150F on Friday and Saturday.

Le Duc des Lombards

42, Rue des Lombards, 75001 (C3)
☎ **01 42 33 22 88**
Metro Châtelet.

Enjoy improvisations, Latin American and French jazz in this lively club. Concerts are at 10pm, 9pm on Sun. Admission is 70F on weekdays, 80F on Fri. and Sat.

Le Baiser Salé

56, Rue des Lombards, 75001 (C3)
☎ **01 42 33 37 71**
Open every day 7pm-6am, jazz at 10pm, Sun. at 9pm.

You'll hear a wide range of jazz from Africa, South America, USA and Europe. There are contemporary French songs at 8pm, Thur., Fri. and Sat, jazz at 10pm. Admission from 30-70E

Le Sunset

60, Rue des Lombards (C3)
☎ **01 40 26 46 60**
Open every day 9.30pm to dawn. Concert at 10pm, 9pm on Sun.

Opened in 1976, this is now the oldest club in the street. Listen to acoustic jazz, predominantly bop, with Christian Vander, the Belmondo Brothers and Laurent de Wilde. On Sundays there's local jazz, Mondays Latin jazz, Tuesdays new generation jazz and you can hear international bands Wednesday to Saturday. Admission from 50-80F.

Le New Morning

7/9, Rue des Petites-Écuries, 75010 (D2)
☎ **01 45 23 51 41**
Metro Château d'Eau
Doors open at 8pm
Concerts at 9pm
Bookings 4.30-7.30pm.

A very popular club, with all the big names in jazz from Art Blakey to Dizzy Gillespie having played here. The decor is reminiscent of a converted garage. Salsa, blues, Afro, rock and a variety of live music. Admission about 110F.

Pubs

Kitty O'Shea

10, Rue des Capucines,
75002 (C3)
☎ 01 40 15 00 30
Metro Opéra.
Open every day noon-1.30am.

A little bit of the Emerald Isle in
Paris, with live satellite TV cover-
age of Irish sporting matches on
Sundays at 3pm. People of all
ages come here at weekends. Live
music on Sunday evenings at
8pm. A whisky costs 35F.

The Frog & Rosbif

116, Rue Saint-Denis,
75002 (C3)
☎ 01 42 36 34 73
Metro Étienne-Marcel
Open every day noon-2am.
This pub is very British indeed,
and English beer is brewed on
the premises. There's a regular
crowd, both French and Anglo-
phone. Acid jazz and funk is
played in a relaxed atmosphere.
A pint costs 35F, and a jug 100F.
Try brunch on Sundays, from
noon until 4pm.

Trendy Parisian Bars

The focus of trendy Parisian
nightlife has recently shifted
towards the 11th *arrondissement*, between République and
Père-Lachaise (D3) and the area
just north of the Place de la
Bastille is really buzzing.

Café-Charbons

109, Rue Oberkampf, 75011
☎ 01 43 57 55 13
Metro Parmentier
Open every day 9am-2am.
Brunch Sat. and Sun. noon-
5pm.

Le Cithéa

114, Rue Oberkampf, 75011
☎ 01 40 21 70 95

La Mercerie

98, Rue Oberkampf
☎ 01 43 38 81 30

Le Troisième Bureau

74, Rue de la Folie-
Méricourt, 75011
☎ 01 43 55 87 65

Le Satellit'café

44, Rue de la Folie-
Méricourt, 75011
☎ 01 47 00 48 87

La Perla

26, Rue François-Miron,
75004 (D4)
☎ 01 42 77 59 40
Metro Saint-Paul.
Oprn every day noon-2am.

Le Camelot

50, Rue Amelot, 75011
☎ 01 43 55 54 04

Le Clown Bar

114, Rue Amelot, 75011
☎ 01 43 55 87 35

Les Couleurs

117, Rue Saint-Maur 75011
☎ 01 43 57 95 61
Metro Parmentier or
Saint-Maur
Open every day 1pm-2am.

At the intersection of Rue
Oberkampf and Rue Saint-Maur,
between the metro stations
Parmentier and Ménilmontant, is
the pulse of Paris nightlife. In the
last few months, several bars have
opened, some of which are already
fashionable, whilst others are less
popular but more gritty. **Les
Couleurs** is worth a visit. Go for
the Tango morning sessions (Sat.)
or the concerts of Swing, jazz and
African music (Fri.-Sun.). The
ambience is great and the clientele artists, actors and students.

Le Cannibale Café

93, Rue Jean-Pierre-
Timbaud at the corner of the
Rue du Moulin-Joli, 75011
☎ 01 49 29 95 59
Metro Couronne
Open every day 7am-2am.
This is an eclectic café which att-
racts a mix of cultures and ages.
Have a brasserie-style lunch with
the arty cinema crowd. The decor
includes chandeliers and mir-
rors. Cocktails cost from 37F.

La Flèche d'Or

102 bis, Rue de Bagnolet
75020 (E3)

FLÈCHE D'OR CAFÉ

☎ 01 43 72 04 23
Metro Gambetta or Porte de
Bagnolet
Open every day 10am-2am,
Mon. 6pm-2am.

The small train no longer runs along the railway line that encircled Paris and ran under the old Bagnolet Station. The track is overgrown with weeds. The station itself, has been converted into a lively bistrot, frequented by local artists and trendies, the young and not-quite-so-young. There's live music on Saturday evenings, and the beer is a lot cheaper than in Montparnasse or at the Bastille. This place is not yet on the tourist trail. Brunch on Sundays is fun.

Le China Club

50, Rue de Charenton,
75012 (D4)
☎ 01 43 43 82 02
Metro Ledru-Rollin
Open every day 7pm-2am,
Fri. & Sat. to 3.30am.

Stepping across the threshold is like stepping into a luxurious club in colonial Hong Kong or Saigon. The first part of the room is the restaurant, but the bar at the back is particularly spectacular, with comfortable sofas, high windows, and an incredibly long counter. It's the perfect place for a romantic Long Island Iced Tea. The bathroom, on the first floor is worth a look. Try the 'smoking room' (more intimate

and cosy than the ground floor, if you don't mind the smoke that is), and listen to an aria or two. It's an exotic and sophisticated change of scene and makes you feel as if you're on a film set.

Lou Pascalou

14, Rue des Panoyaux,
75020 (E4)
(01 46 36 78 10
Metro Ménilmontant

This old bistrot is open every day 8am-2am, and has recently been rejuvenated. Its decor is straight out of a post-war realist movie and remains, however, quite unchanged. It's a favourite haunt of young artists and budding actors who come here to enjoy the is a friendly, relaxed atmosphere. You can even have a game of French billiards. A good spot for an evening drink

Le Soleil

136, Boulevard de
Ménilmontant 75020 (E4)
☎ 01 46 36 47 44
Metro Ménilmontant.
Open every day 9am-2am.

In Paris, news of the latest 'in' places travels on the grapevine, and things tends to change fast. Go to the Soleil for an apéritif before it goes out of fashion. It has a colourful clientèle with people from all walks of life. In the evenings the large terrace is full of young people from all over Paris who come to relax and drink a (cheap) beer or a Ricard. It's the kind of place where someone is likely to start playing a guitar, and has a relaxed and friendly atmosphere.

Les Portes

15, Rue de Charonne
75011 (D4)
☎ 01 40 21 70 61
Metro Bastille
Open every day noon-
midnight, Sun 5pm-
midnight.

The cosy, intimate little bar here is absolutely perfect for a 'tête-à-tête'. You'll soon feel at home in this warm and inviting place with its odd pieces of furniture and good music. It's ideal for a drink late on a winter afternoon, or for an apéritif while you wait for a table in one of the nearby restaurants. There's a little outdoors terrace with tables in the summer, where you can sit and watch the world go by. There are good salads at lunchtime.

La Liberté

196, Rue du faubourg Saint-
Antoine 75012 Paris (E4)
☎ 01 43 72 11 18
Metro Faidherbe-Chaligny
Open every day 9am-2am.

There was nothing special about this local bistrot until a change

NOUVEAU SPECTACLE
C'EST MAGIQUE !

LIDO
de Paris

Cabarets and revues

Welcome to the world of cabaret. If you're looking for some high kicks, try the following venues:

La Belle Époque
36, Rue des Petits-Champs, 75002
☎ 01 42 96 33 33

Crazy Horse
12, Ave George-V, 75008
☎ 01 47 23 32 32

Le Lido
116 bis, Ave des Champs-Élysées, 75008
☎ 01 40 76 56 10

Chez Michou
80, Rue des Martyrs, 75018
☎ 01 46 06 16 04

Le Paradis Latin
28, Rue du Cardinal-Lemoine, 75005
☎ 01 43 25 28 28

Satellit Café
44, Rue de la Folie-Méricourt, 75011 (D3)
☎ 01 47 00 48 87
Metro Oberkampf, Parmentier, Saint-Ambroise
Open Mon.-Thur. 6pm-2am, Fri. & Sat. 6pm-dawn.

This place is timeless rather than trendy and is open to those aged 18 to infinity. Old vinyl record jackets decorate the walls, and you sit on black iron chairs at copper tables. Listen to rock, Flamenco, Cuban or Tibetan music and French songs. Drinks cost 35-68F and you can dance if you're in the mood.

Dance bars

Le Cithéa
114, Rue Oberkampf, 75011 (D3)
☎ 01 42 33 28 73
Metro Ménilmontant
Call for concert information.

The interior of this bar is classical but still modern and the clientèle is quite up-market. After the concert, which can be rock, jazz, or pop, a DJ takes over and gets everyone on the dance floor. It's not obligatory – you can just have a drink if you're not in the mood.

La Casbah
23, Rue de la Forge-Royale, 75011 (D4)
☎ 01 43 71 71 89
Metro Ledru-Rollin, Faidherbe-Chaligny
Open every day, bar from 8pm, disco Thur. & Fri. at 11pm.

Ties are not essential, but there is a bouncer at the door. The decor is Moroccan and the music, acid jazz with an Oriental flavour. There's belly dancing at 11pm Fri.-Sat. Admission with a drink costs 120F. A second drink is 50F.

Le Moloko
26, Rue Fontaine, 75009 (C2)
☎ 01 48 74 50 26

of management turned it into a great little café. The clientèle has changed too and is now young and trendy, but less pretentious than at the Bastille. There's live music on Saturday nights. You can play chess and backgammon here on other nights. Pop in for a drink and a game.

Metro Pigalle
Open every day 9.30pm-6am.

On the ground floor, there's a juke-box with a choice of 100 CDs to dance to. There's another bar upstairs, which is open at weekends. It has paintings based on the theme of 'woman', a red velvet decor, and performances on a mini-stage by actors or musicians. It's happy hour till 1am, with beer for 15F, spirits for 20F. Outside happy hour, beer costs 35F and spirits cost 50F.

What's Up

15, Rue Daval, 75011 (D4)
☎ 01 48 05 88 33
Metro Bastille
Open every day to 7pm-2am
Show starts at 10pm.

This is a gigantic, spacious bar, with atmospheric soft lighting. Groove, new-jack, soul and acid jazz start 11pm. What's Up nights

Late-night dining

You can find anything in Paris, including restaurants open 24 hours a day.
L'Alsace aux Halles, 16, Rue Coquillère, 75001, ☎ 01 42 36 74 24.
Cosmos Café, 101, Blvd Montparnasse, 75006, ☎ 01 43 26 74 36.
Le Grand Café Capucines, 4, Blvd des Capucines, 75009, ☎ 01 43 12 19 00.
La Maison d'Alsace, 39, Ave des Champs Élysées, ☎ 01 53 93 97 00.
Au Pied de Cochon, 6, Rue Coquillère, 75001, ☎ 01 40 13 77 00.
Pub Saint-Germain, 17, Rue de l'Ancienne-Comédie, 75006, ☎ 01 43 29 38 70.

take place every Friday and Saturday, with a DJ. Don't wear anything too outrageous. The decor is by a designer who worked with Philipe Starck. Happy hour operates from 8-10.30pm, 20-45F (after 10.30pm, 30-55F). Thur.-Sat. admission (including drink) is 50F.

Nightclubs

Queen

102, Avenue des Champs-Élysées, 75008 (A3)
☎ 01 53 89 08 90
Metro Charles-de-Gaulle-Étoile
Open every night from midnight.

This is the city's most fashionable nightclub, even though it's theoretically a gay club. Every Friday is 'Made in Queen' night, with a different international DJ every week. There are disco nights on Mondays and shows take place every evening. On Fri.-Sun. admission is 100F with a drink, 50F on Monday, free on other nights. Don't bother arriving before midnight or 1am. If you only have one night to spare, this is the place to go.

Les Bains

7, Rue du Bourg-l'Abbé, 75003 (C3)
☎ 01 48 87 01 80
Metro Étienne Marcel.
Open every day 10pm-dawn, Restaurant: 8.30pm-1am.

Jonathan Amar designed the Baroque interior (red, gold and burgundy) of this temple of the night, where the beautiful people mix with visiting celebrities.

If you come with a regular or have an invitation, you'll have no difficulty getting in. Otherwise it's best to try your luck as a couple. There's all kinds of music, including World and groove. Admission is 100F Mon.-Thur., 140F Fri. and Sat., including drink. A Second drink costs 100F

Le Bal, Élysée Montmartre

72, Blvd de Rochechouart, 75018 (C2)
☎ 01 42 52 76 84
Metro Anvers
11pm-5am every other Sat.

This is a cross between a local dance and a disco, with all kinds of music played by the Élysée Montmartre band or the DJ. There's a mixed crowd of all ages and plenty of 'golden oldies'. Don't be in too much of a hurry to get in, it's very popular. Admission is 80F, drinks from 25-40F.

Le Balajo

9, Rue de Lappe, 75011 (D4)
☎ 01 47 00 07 87
Metro Bastille
Open Wed.-Sat. 11.30pm-5.30am, afternoon ballroom dancing Sat. & Sun. 3-6.30pm
Entry charge 50F.

Entry charge: 50F. Enjoy Zazou swing on Wednesday nights, rock and Cuban on Thursdays, rock and swing on Fridays and Saturdays. Admission is 100F including a drink.

Understanding the menu

Understanding the menu can cause problems, so this handy translator should help you decide what to order. Bon appetit!

le plat du jour
dish of the day

la carte des vins
wine list

la formule/le menu à prix fixe
fixed price menu

le couvert
cover charge

DRINKS

un orange/citron pressé
fresh orange/lemon juice

un express
espresso coffee

un café noir
black coffee

un café-crème
coffee with steamed milk

un café décaféine
decaffeinated coffee

un thé
tea

au lait/au citron
with milk/lemon

du sucre
some sugar

tisane/infusion
herbal tea

SUNDRIES

le petit pain
bread roll

les pâtes
pasta

le riz
rice

un oeuf
egg

COOKING STYLES

cuit(e) au four
baked

grillé(e)
grilled

bouilli(e)
boiled

poché(e)
poached

poêlé(e)
pan-fried

à la vapeur
steamed

MEAT

le gibier
game

l'entrecôte/le steak/le bifteck
steak

le jambon
ham

les rognons
kidneys

le veau
veal

le lapin
rabbit

la saucisse
sausage

les cuisses de grenouilles
frogs' legs

les escargots
snails

SEAFOOD

les fruits de mer
seafood

les crustaces
shellfish

le cabillaud/morue
cod

le saumon (fumé)
salmon (smoked)

le hareng
herring

le brochet
pike

le thon
tuna

la truite
trout

le bar
sea bass

le rouget
red mullet

la raie
skate

le calmar
squid

les huitres
oysters

les moules
mussels

les crevettes
prawns

le homard
lobster

la langoustine
Dublin bay prawn/scampi

VEGETABLES

pommes de terre
potatoes

chou
cabbage

chou-fleur
cauliflower

choucroute
sauerkraut

petits pois
peas

haricots verts
green beans

épinards
spinach

poireaux
leeks

l'ail
garlic

poivron/poivron rouge
green/red pepper

betterave
beetroot

la salade frisée
curly endive

FRUIT

pomme
apple

poire
pear

orange
orange

citron
lemon

raisins
grapes

fraises
strawberries

framboises
raspberries

prunes/mirabelles
plums

groseilles
red/white currants

cassis
blackcurrants

mûres
blackberries

pêches
peaches

cerises
cherries

DESSERTS/ CHEESE

glace
ice cream

crème fraiche
cream

gâteau
cake

tarte aux pommes
apple tart

fromage de chèvre
goat's cheese

Conversion tables for clothes shopping

Women's sizes

Shirts/dresses

U.K	U.S.A	EUROPE
8	6	36
10	8	38
12	10	40
14	12	42
16	14	44
18	16	46

Sweaters

U.K	U.S.A	EUROPE
8	6	44
10	8	46
12	10	48
14	12	50
16	14	52

Shoes

U.K	U.S.A	EUROPE
3	5	36
4	6	37
5	7	38
6	8	39
7	9	40
8	10	41

Men's sizes

Shirts

U.K	U.S.A	EUROPE
14	14	36
$14^{1}/_{2}$	$14^{1}/_{2}$	37
15	15	38
$15^{1}/_{2}$	$15^{1}/_{2}$	39
16	16	41
$16^{1}/_{2}$	$16^{1}/_{2}$	42
17	17	43
$17^{1}/_{2}$	$17^{1}/_{2}$	44
18	18	46

Suits

U.K	U.S.A	EUROPE
36	36	46
38	38	48
40	40	50
42	42	52
44	44	54
46	46	56

Shoes

U.K	U.S.A	EUROPE
6	8	39
7	9	40
8	10	41
9	10.5	42
10	11	43
11	12	44
12	13	45

More useful conversions

1 centimetre	0.39 inches	1 inch	2.54 centimetres
1 metre	1.09 yards	1 yard	0.91 metres
1 kilometre	0.62 miles	1 mile	1. 61 kilometres
1 litre	1.76 pints	1 pint	0.57 litres
1 gram	0.35 ounces	1 ounce	28.35 grams
1 kilogram	2.2 pounds	1 pound	0.45 kilograms

This guide was written by **Catherine Synave**, with the assistance of **Betty der Andreassian**. This edition was updated by **Frédérique Pélissier** and **Pétronille Danchin**. Copy editor: **Elizabeth Ayre**. Translated by **Lisa Davidson**. Revision of English edition **Jane Moseley** and **Vanessa Byrne**. Series editor **Liz Coghill**.

We have done our best to ensure the accuracy of the information contained in this guide. However, addresses, phone numbers, opening times etc. inevitably do change from time to time, so if you find a discrepancy please do let us know. You can contact us at: hachetteuk@orionbooks.co.uk or write to us at Hachette UK, address below.

Hachette UK guides provide independent advice. The authors and compilers do not accept any remuneration for the inclusion of any addresses in these guides.

Please note that we cannot accept any responsibility for any loss, injury or inconvenience sustained by anyone as a result of any information or advice contained in this guide.

Photo acknowledgements
Inside: **Christian Sarramon** : pp. 2 (t.c.), 3 (t.l., c.a., b.l., b.r.), 8 (t.r., c.l.), 9 (t.r., c.l. background, c.l. foreground), 10 (t.r.), 11 (t.c., c.r., b.), 12 (c., b.), 13, 14, 15 (b.l.), 16 (t.r., c.r., b.r.), 17, 18 (t.r., c.r.), 19 (b.c.), 20, 21, 25 (t.r.), 26 (c.l., c.r.), 27, 31, 32, 34 (c.r., b.l.), 35 (c.l., b.r.), 36 (c.r., b.), 37 (t.c., c.r., b.r.), 38 (b.l., b.r.), 39, 40 (b.l.), 41, 42 (c.r.), 43 (c.b., b.r.), 44, 45 (t.c., b.l. rights reserved, b.c.), 46, 47 (c.c., b.r.), 48, 49 (c.l., b.r.), 50 (b.l.), 51, 52, 53 (c.l., c.c., b.r.), 54 (c.), 55 (rights reserved), 56, 57, 58, 59 (t.l., c., b.r.), 61, 62, 63, 64, 65 (t.c., c.r., b.r.), 68 (c.b., b.r.), 69, 71 (t., c.r.), 77, 78 (t.l., b.l., b.r.), 79 (c., b.c.), 85 (t.r.), 86 (c.), 87 (c. b.), 90(t.r., c. foreground and background), 93 (t., c.l.), 94 (b.r.), 95 (c.r., b.l.), 96 (t.c., 97 (c.r., b.), 103 (c.t.r., c. b.), 104 (c.b., c.r.), 107, 108 (t.c., c.r.), 109 (t.r.), 110, 111 (c.l., b.r.), 113 (t.l., t.c., b. g.), 114 (c.l., c.b.), 115 (t.l., b.l.), 122 (t.c.), 124 (c.r.). **Marc Michiels** : pp. 12 (t.), 15 (t.r.), 85 (c.l., b.r.), 112 (c., c.r., b.), 113 (c.r., b.r.) 114 (t.r., b.r.), 115 (t.c., c.r., b.r., b.c.); **Peter Tebbitt** : pp. 11 (t.r.), 33 (c.l.), 35 (c.l.), 36 (b.l.), 42 (t., b.l. rights reserved), 50 (b.r.), 60 (b.l.), 65 (c.l.), 68 (c.l.); **I. Rozenbaum/F. Cirou, Photo Alto** : pp. 8-9 (b.), 19 (c.l., c.r.), 34 (c.l.), 112 (t.r.), 118; **Pawel Wysocki** : 46 (c.l.); **Laurent Parrault** : pp. 91 (c.), 93 (b.), 94 (t.); **Éric Guillot** : p. 59 (t.l.); **Hachette** : pp. 10 (b.), 15 (b.), 18 (c.l.), 22 (c.r.), 26 (t.r., b.), 35 (c.r.), 38 (c.l.), 43 (c.l.), 109 (c.r.); **Rights reserved** : pp. 33 (t.l.), 42 (c.r.), 121 (t.c., c.l.), 122 (t.l.); ©**Orop (Le Procope)** : p. 16 (c.l.); **Lenôtre** : p. 18 (b.); **Fauchon** : pp. 19 (t.), 111 (t.r.); © **Christian Lacroix** : pp. 22 (t.l., b.c.), 23 (b.r.); **Christian Louboutin** : p. 23 (t.r.); **Vuitton** : pp. 23 (c.l.), 25 (c.l.); © **Chanel/Mademoiselle Chanel par Hoyningen Huene 1935** : p. 24 (c.l.); **Puiforcat**/© **Arcadia** : p. 24 (c.r.) **Guerlain** : pp. 24 (t.r.), 84 (c.l.); **Hermès**/© **F. Dumas** : pp. 24 (b.r.), 37 (c.l.); **Prunier** : p. 34 (c.); **Bernardaud** : pp. 37 (c.c.), 100 (b.); **Anna Joliet** : p. 40 (c.l.); **Bonpoint** : pp. 45 (c.r.), 95 (t.r.); **Shu Uemura** : p. 47 (t.l.); **Ch. Tortu** : p. 49 (t.c.); **Le Vieux Campeur**/© **T.-J. Oremusz** : p. 53 (c.r.); **Café Beaubourg** : p. 54 (b.r.); **Opéra Bastille** : p. 65 (c.l.); **Le Pavillon de la Reine** : p. 70 (c.). **Hôtel Caron de Beaumarchais** : p. 70 (c.r.); **Hôtel Saint-Dominique** : p. 71 (b.r.) **Hôtel Franklin Roosevelt** : p. 72; **Hôtel Galileo** : p. 73 (t.l.); **Hôtel Tronchet** : p. 73 (b.l.); **Hôtel Pergolèse** : p. 73 (b.r.); **Le Grand Colbert** : p. 74 (c.l., b.); **Ambassade d'Auvergne** : p. 74 (c.r.); **Brasserie des Musées** : p. 76; **Lapérouse:** p. 78 (c.r.); **Lucas-Carton:** p. 79 (c.l.); **La Closerie des Lilas**/© **Phototypie l'Abeille**: p. 79 (t., c.r.); **Fermette Marbeuf**/© **H. Boutet**: p. 79 (b.r.); **Benneton** : p. 84 (b.l.), 103; **Poilâne** : p. 84 (c.r.); **Androuët** : p. 85 (t.l.); **Lolita Lempicka**/© **F. Dumoulin** : p. 86 (t.r.), 87 (t.l.); **GAP**/© **G. Matoso** : p. 86 (c.l.); **Schinichiro Arakawa** : p. 86 (b.r.) **Martin Grant** : p. 87 (c.r.); **Doria Salambo** : p. 87 (b.r.); **Axes et Loisirs** : p. 88 (c.r.); **Anne Fontaine** : p. 88 (b.l.) **Total Éclipse** : p. 88 (t.r.); **Upla** : p. 88 (t.r.); **Big Ben Club** : p. 88 (t.l.); **Bleu Forêt** : p. 89 (b.l.); **Camper** : p. 89 (t.r., c.); **Mosquitos**/© **Univers Presse** : p. 89 (b.); **Lionel Nath** : p. 100 (b.l.); **Timberland** : p. 91 (c., b.), 108 (b.); **Bain Plus** : p. 92 (c.r., b.r.); **Atomica**/© **J. L Cagnin** : p. 91 (t.c.); **La Cerise sur le Gâteau** : p. 94 (c.l.); **Croissant** : p. 95 (t.l.); **Avant Scène** : p. 96 (c.); **Globe Trotter** : p. 96 (b.l.); **Conceptua** : p. 96 (t.r.); **Agnès Comar** : p. 97 (c.l.); **Laure Japy** : p. 98 (t.l.); **Bodum**/© **J. Polony** : p. 98 (t.c.); **A la mine d'argent** : p. 99 (t.); **La Tisanière** : p. 99 (c.l.); **La Maison Ivre** : p. 101 (t.l.); **Salle Pleyel** : p. 119 (b.); © **Florian Kleinefenn/Sipa Press** : p. 120 (t.); **Le Bar de la Villa**/© **P. Bogner** : p. 120 (c.); **Flèche d'Or Café** : p. 121 (b.); **Lido**: p. 123; **Au Pied de Cochon** : p. 124 (c.l.); **Le Queen** : p. 124 (c., c.); **Taïr Mercier** : p. 101 (b.r.); **Paris-Musées** : p. 101 (c., b.); **Artistes et Modèles** : p. 102 (t., b.r.); **Michèle Wilson** : p. 102 (c.); **Axis**/© **V. Grenuillet** : p. 103 (b.l.); **C.F.O.C.** : p. 104 (c.l.); **Galerie Urubamba** : p. 105; **Matins Bleus** : p. 106 (t., c.); **Surcouf** : p. 109 (b.l.); **Olsen Bornholm** : p. 111 (c.), **Bateaux parisiens** : p. 119; © **Nicolas Borel** *Front cover:* **Ch. Sarramon** : t.l., c.c., c.r., b.l., b.r; **M. Michiels** : t.r., c.l.; **Image Bank/David de Lossy**: c.r. (figures) **Pix/Ling Bill** : t. (figures); **Fotogram-Stone/Chris Craymer** : b. (figure) *Back cover:* **Ch. Sarramon** : t.r., b.l **M. Michiels** : c.r; **Rights reserved** : c.l.

Illustrations Pascal Garnier   **Cartography** © Hachette Tourisme

First published in the United Kingdom in 2000 by Hachette UK

© English Translation, revised and updated, Hachette UK 2000
© Hachette Livre (Hachette Tourisme) 1999

Distributed in the United States of America by Sterling Publishing Co., Inc.
387 Park Avenue South, New York, NY 10016-8810

A CIP catalogue for this book is available from the British Library

ISBN 1 84202 001 3

Hachette UK, Cassell & Co., The Orion Publishing Group, Wellington House, 125 Strand, London WC2R 0BB

Printed and bound in Italy by Vincenzo Bona

If you're staying longer than a weekend and want to discover new places, the following pages should provide you with a choice of hotels, restaurants and bars classified by *arrondissement* or quarter. Though you may be able to turn up at most restaurants and get a table (except the most up-market ones), you should try and book in advance (see p. 66). Enjoy your stay.

STAYING ON A LITTLE LONGER

This list of hotels is classified by *arrondissement* (quarter) and selected on the basis of its location and value for money. Prices given are for a double room with en-suite bathroom or shower. We have given a price range, which is subject to change. Unless indicated, free parking is not available at the hotel. Room tax (*taxe de séjour*) and breakfast are not included. Room tax is usually 6/7F per person per night and breakfast is anything from 30-55F. For further information on hotels in Paris see p. 66.

1st arrondissement

Hôtel Louvre-Forum**
25, Rue de Bouloi
☎ 01 42 36 54 19
✆ 01 42 33 66 31
Metro Palais Royal-Musée du Louvre
400-540F

This hotel is a stone's throw from the gardens of the Palais Royal, the Louvre Museum and the Forum des Halles and is close to several bus stops and metro stations. It has two reception rooms and a private bar. Breakfast is served in a vaulted cellar. The 27 rooms all have mini-bars. Parking nearby.

Hôtel des Victoires***
19, Rue Hérold
☎ 01 42 36 04 02
✆ 01 45 08 14 09
Metro Louvre-Rivoli or Les Halles
580-620F.

You'll enjoy excellent service at this quiet 29-room hotel located near the Hôtel des Victoires, the Louvre, the Palais Royal and Les Halles. The terrace is open in the summer months.

2nd arrondissement

Hôtel François
3, Bd Montmartre
☎ 01 42 33 51 53
✆ 01 40 26 29 90
Metro Rue Montmartre
990-1650F.

This is the ideal hotel if you're in Paris on a shopping trip, as the large department stores on Boulevard Haussmann (Printemps, Galeries Lafayette, Marks and Spencer...) are just minutes away.

3rd arrondissement

Hôtel Paris France**
72, Rue de Tubirgo
☎ 01 42 78 00 04 and
01 42 78 64 92
✆ 01 42 71 99 43
Metro République
450F.

This hotel was fully renovated in 1998 and each of the 46 rooms has a safe. Located in the heart of the Marais quarter, near Beaubourg, the hotel is conveniently near the République metro station.

5th arrondissement

Hotel d'Alba***
1, Rue de la Harpe
☎ 01 46 34 09 70
✆ 01 40 46 85 70
Metro Saint-Michel or Cluny
670-825 FF.

This hotel, with 45 recently renovated rooms, is ideally situated in the heart of the Latin Quarter (near Notre-Dame, the Seine and the Louvre). NB This is a very lively area at night

6th arrondissement

Hotel Delhy's*
22, Rue de l'Hirondelle
☎ 01 43 26 58 25
✆ 01 43 26 51 06
Metro Saint-Michel
290-380F.

This hotel is a good base from which to explore the Latin Quarter, Notre-Dame, the Louvre and the Musée d'Orsay on foot. The nearby Saint-Michel métro and RER will take you to other arrondissements in minutes. This hotel has 21 rooms, great service and a friendly family ambiance.

Grand Hôtel des Balcons**
3, Rue Casimir Delavigne
☎ 01 46 34 78 50
✆ 01 46 34 06 27
Metro Odéon or Luxembourg
495-530F.

Situated in a small street between Odéon and the Saint-Michel and Saint-Germain boulevards, this charming hotel still has an Art Nouveau decor, with original 1900s woodwork and stained-glass windows. If it is your birthday during your stay, they will offer you a free buffet breakfast. It's excellent value for money.

7th arrondissement

Grand Hôtel Lévêque*
29, Rue Cler
☎ 01 47 05 49 15
✆ 01 45 50 49 36
Metro École Militaire or la Tour Maubourg
380-400F.

It may sound a contradiction in terms, but this is a one-star luxury hotel, with great prices as well as service and facilities. The rooms have been recently renovated, and there is a drinks dispenser in the lobby. The location is ideal as the hotel is on a lively pedestrian street with a busy market and is just minutes away from the Eiffel Tower and the Champs-Élysées.

Hôtel de Nevers**
83, Rue du Bac
☎ 01 45 44 61 30
✆ 01 42 22 29 47
Metro Rue du Bac
470-530F.

This hotel is situated in a renovated 18th-century building in the heart of Saint-Germain-des-Prés, near several restaurants, antique shops and fashion boutiques. Parking available nearby. The Eiffel Tower and the Louvre are both within walking distance.

8th arrondissement

Hôtel Marigny**
11, Rue de l'Arcade
☎ 01 42 66 42 71
✆ 01 47 42 06 76
Metro Madeleine
510F.

Leave your car in one of the car parks near the hotel, and discover the charm of the Madeleine quarter, which leads on to the Opéra, the department stores, the Rue Royale and Place de la Concorde. This hotel has 32 rooms, all with mini-bars, and a pleasant lobby.

9th arrondissement

Hôtel Monnier★★
14, Rue Henry-Monnier
☎ 01 42 85 37 19
📠 01 42 85 24 73
Metro Saint-Georges
360F, including breakfast.
This hotel is situated in a quiet, residential area near Sacré Cœur and close to several métro lines running to the major tourist sites in Paris.

12th arrondissement

Lux-Hôtel★★
8, Av. de Corbéra
☎ 01 43 43 42 84
📠 01 43 43 14 45
Metro Gare de Lyon
300-350F.
The Bastille Opera, the Jardin des Plantes and the trendy bars on Rue de Lappe are all within walking distance. The staff are friendly, and you'll get good service at a good price.

Hôtel Aurore
13, Rue Traversière
☎ 01 43 43 54 12
📠 01 43 43 53 20
Metro Gare de Lyon
490-510F.
This fully renovated hotel has excellent facilities, 30 rooms with cable TV, hair dryers, automatic alarm clocks and a pleasant breakfast room with exposed stonework.

14th arrondissement

Hôtel Celtic★
15, Rue d'Odessa
☎ 01 43 20 93 53 or
01 43 20 83 91
📠 01 43 20 66 07
Metro Montparnasse or Edgar Quinet
280-300F.
A comfortable hotel situated behind the Montparnasse station in a lively neighbourhood with lots of restaurants and cinemas. Parking nearby.

Hôtel Delambre★★★
35, Rue Delambre
☎ 01 43 20 66 31
📠 01 45 38 91 76
Metro Montparnasse, Vavin or Edgar Quinet
460-550F.
Situated in the heart of Montparnasse, a few metro stops from Saint-Germain-des-Prés and the Latin Quarter, this hotel has quiet, modern rooms and a breakfast buffet. In the evening, enjoy a stroll in the nearby Luxembourg gardens.

15th arrondissement

Hôtel Alizé-Grenelle★★★
87, Av. Émile-Zola
☎ 01 45 78 08 22
📠 01 40 59 03 06
Metro Charles-Michels
430-530F.
This is a modern hotel in the heart of the Beaugrenelle business district, located a short metro ride from the Eiffel Tower. Each of the 50 rooms has a mini-bar and a trouser press. The hotel also has a conference room (catering for 15 to 20 people) and a pleasant lobby. Breakast is served in your room, or in the dining room. Parking nearby.

Hôtel Beaugrenelle Saint-Charles★★
82, Rue Saint-Charles
☎ 01 45 78 61 63
📠 01 45 79 04 38
Metro Charles-Michels
420-520F.
The hotel has 51 rooms, all equipped with a trouser press and a mini-bar. It also caters for conferences (up to 20 people), and has a private garden. In the heart of the business district, and not too far from the Eiffel Tower, Trocadéro and, a little further, the Bois de Boulogne.

16th arrondissement

Au Palais de Chaillot★★
35, Av. Raymond-Poincaré
☎ 01 53 70 09 09
📠 01 53 70 09 08
Metro Trocadéro or Victor Hugo
530-590F.

HOTELS

You can walk from this hotel to the Eiffel Tower, the Arc de Triomphe and the Champs-Élysées. From the nearby Trocadéro and Victor Hugo metro stations, you can reach the centre of Paris in minutes. The business centres at the Palais des Congrès and the Défense are also nearby. Rooms are equipped for portable computers and a laundry service is available.

18th arrondissement

Hôtel Montmartrois★★
6 bis, Rue du Chevalier-de-la-Barre
☎ 01 53 41 84 40 or
01 42 54 86 90
☎ 01 42 57 02 33
Metro Jules Joffrin or
Château Rouge
300F.
This hotel is perched high on the Montmartre hill behind the Sacré Cœur church in a small, picturesque street. It has 95 rooms and apartments, and guests can use a fully equipped kitchen or kitchenette plus a conference room for 20–30 people. Parking nearby.

Hôtel Regyn's Montmartre★★
18, Pl. des Abbesses
☎ 01 42 54 45 21
☎ 01 42 23 76 69
Metro Abbesses
445F.
The 22 rooms in this hotel have been recently renovated and all now have a radio and a safe. Situated in the heart of Montmartre, the hotel is in a great location. For just 10F more per person, you can have a room with a spectacular view over Paris. Parking nearby (100F/24 hours).

19th arrondissement

Hôtel du Parc des Buttes Chaumont★★★
1, Pl. Armand-Carrel
☎ 01 42 08 08 37
☎ 01 42 45 66 91
Metro Laumière
460-500F.
This hotel near the Cité de la Villette is in a lovely setting. The 45 rooms either overlook the Parc des Buttes Chaumont or the private garden. You can use the private parking facilities (45F per night or 75F/24 hours), enjoy a delicious buffet-style breakfast and play board games or billiards in the lobby. The hotel hires out the reception rooms for special events, seminars and cocktail parties.

20th arrondissement

Palma★★
77, Av. Gambetta
☎ 01 46 36 13 65
☎ 01 46 36 03 27
Metro Gambetta
370-425F.
Recently renovated, this hotel has 32 light and well insulated rooms, each with television (foreign language programmes are available, including English). Breakfast is served in your room or in the dining room. It's well situated near public transport and you can park opposite the hotel.

HOTELS

France is a gastronomic paradise and offers a tremendous range of food from all over the world. We have selected restaurants serving different styles of cuisine, among them Chinese, Japanese, Indian, and, of course, French. You'll find cafés, brasseries, bistrots and luxurious restaurants for those very special occasions. Bon appetit!

INTERNATIONAL CUISINES

1st arrondissement

IRISH

Carr's
1, Rue du Mont Thabor
☎ 01 42 60 60 26
Metro Tuileries
Open evenings.
Fixed-price menus:
70-145F et à la carte.
Don't try to order wine here; all they serve is beer, and most of it's Irish. Irish bands play on Friday and Saturday nights. This is a great place to take a break after a stroll through the Tuileries Gardens.

3th arrondissement

SPANISH

Les Caves St-Gilles
4, Rue St-Gilles
☎ 01 48 87 22 62
Metro Chemin Vert
Open daily except
Dec. 25 and Jan. 1,
8am-1.30am.
À la carte: 80-120F.
If you feel like an authentic Spanish meal, try this restaurant, where you'll find platefuls of hot and cold tapas, a wonderful decor and a great Spanish ambiance. It is small and almost always full, so it's advisable to book ahead.

6th arrondissement

GREEK

Zorba
14, Rue Grégoire de Tours
☎ 01 43 25 26 66
Metro Odéon, Mabillon
Open daily for lunch and dinner to 2am.
Fixed-price menus:
70-125F.
Greek specialities are served under the watchful eye of a photo of Anthony Quinn in his role as Zorba. At night, musicians and dancers entertain the clientèle.

JAPANESE

Kiotori
61, Rue Monsieur le Prince
☎ 01 43 54 48 44
Metro Luxembourg
Open daily for lunch and dinner
Fixed-price menus:
35-100F.
The menu has a wide selection of sushi, chicken and beef brochettes. The prices are reasonable and the restaurant is situated just minutes from the Luxembourg Gardens. It's a pleasant place to stop after visiting the Latin Quarter.

8th arrondissement

TIBETAN

Le Singe d'Eau
28, Rue de Moscou
☎ 01 43 87 72 73
Metro Rome
Open Mon.-Sat. for lunch and dinner. Closed Aug.
Fixed-price menus:
65-100F.
This restaurant opened during the year of the water monkey, according to Chinese astrology, though the food is emphatically Tibetan. Try the violet-flavored lassi or the unusual spiced tea to accompany your meal.

11th arrondissement

MEXICAN

Taco Loco
116, Rue Amelot
☎ 01 43 57 90 24
Metro Oberkampf or Filles du Calvaire
Open daily for lunch and dinner (closed Sun. and Mon. for lunch)
À la carte: 40- 50F
Everything here is authentically Mexican, the decor, the chef and the staff, not to mention the cuisine, which has an extra touch that makes it stand out from the usual Mexican food.

ASIAN

New Nioulaville
32, Rue de l'Orillon
☎ 01 40 21 96 18
40- 50F Belleville
Open daily for lunch and dinner
À la carte: 20-80F.
A waiter comes by the tables with a platter, from which you select your dish. The restaurant offers specialities from all over Asia.

12th arrondissement

SPANISH

La Feria
25, Rue Montgallet
☎ 01 43 41 15 72
40- 50F Montgallet
Open daily for lunch and dinner
Fixed-price menus:
69-138F.
As soon as you walk through the door, you find yourself in an authentic Spanish ambiance, with paintings of bullfights on the walls, cured ham hanging from the ceiling, and a large selection of hot and cold tapas.

13th arrondissement

MOROCCAN

Au Petit Cahoua
39, Bd St-Marcel
☎ 01 47 07 24 42
Metro St-Marcel
Open daily for lunch and dinner (closed Sat. lunch)
About 165F.
This place looks more like a Berber tent than a restaurant. The dining room is decorated with ceramics and has lamps made of stretched hide. Try the chef's speciality, a delicious lamb tajine with pear and acacia honey.

CHINESE

Sinorama
135, Av. de Choisy
☎ 01 44 24 27 81
Metro Tolbiac or Place d'Italie
Open for dinner until 2am.
À la carte: 40-90F.
After exploring the Tang Frères shop, try this restaurant in the heart of Chinatown in the 13th arrondissement for authentic Chinese cuisine. Most of your fellow diners will be Chinese. Don't miss the steamed fish and fantastic duck dishes.

14th arrondissement

GREEK

Télémaque
15, Rue Roger
☎ 01 43 20 66 38
Metro Denfert-Rochereau or Raspail
Open Mon.-Sat. for lunch and dinner; Sun. with reservations. Closed Aug.
Lunch menu: 60-115F,
À la carte (Mon.-Fri.): 55-95F .
This restaurant is run by a Greek couple. You can choose from a menu with dishes ranging from the famous fricassee (lamb with salad), a traditional Greek dish served at Easter, to dolmas, courgette (zucchini) fritters and suckling pig. The pastries are home-made. The room at the back is reserved for non-smokers.

17th arrondissement

INDIAN

Gangotri
18, Rue Lemercier
☎ 01 44 70 04 61
Metro Place de Clichy
Open daily for lunch and dinner (closed Mon. lunch)
Fixed-price menus: 45-99F, à la carte: 100F.
The chef is from northern India, and concocts tandoori and curry specialities. Accompany your meal with Indian wine or beer, or perhaps mango or rose tea. Take-away food is also available.

18th arrondissement

INDIAN

Chez Sonia
8, Rue Letort
01 42 57 23 17
Metro Jules Joffrin
Open daily noon-2pm, 7.30-11pm (closed Sun. lunch)
À la carte: 100F.
Indian restaurants are still quite a rarity in Paris. Start with the Pakora shrimp or chicken Tikka, follow this with the house speciality, the 'Sonia' chicken, served with a cheese nan, but forget the wine. Order an Indian beer or a tea instead.

FRENCH CUISINE

1st arrondissement

Café Véry
Jardin des Tuileries
☎ 01 47 03 94 84
Metro Concorde, Tuileries
Open daily noon-11pm
À la carte: 100-120F.
If you're exploring the Tuileries Gardens and want to have lunch, take a seat in this pleasant café with unusual dishes combining sweet and sour flavours. Try the salmon with coconut sauce, chicken with honey and raisins, or salmon with cucumber and mint. On sunny days the glass doors are opened and you can enjoy both the sun and the view.

2nd arrondissement

Le Tire-Bouchon
22, Rue Tiquetonne
☎ 01 42 21 95 51
Metro Étienne Marcel
Open daily
À la carte: 120F.
The menu changes every day, depending on what the chef selects at the market. This former Parisian bistrot, decorated with old-fashioned murals, serves dishes from Lyon.

RESTAURANTS

5th arrondissement

Trois A
14, Rue Linné
☎ 01 55 43 92 18
Metro Jussieu
Open Mon.-Thur. 11am-3pm, 6-8pm, Fri. 11am-3pm, Sat. 11am-2pm.
15-30F
It's hard to find a good and inexpensive quick lunch in this area, but this is a great place. The entrance is small, but the sandwiches are enormous. If you're really hungry, try one of the maxi-sandwiches, which are the size of half a baguette. Sandwich in hand, walk to the nearby Jardin des Plantes and enjoy a picnic in the sun.

Chantairelle
17, Rue Laplace
☎ 01 46 33 18 59
Metro Cardinal Lemoine
Daily (except Sat. lunch and Sun), open Sun. in summer.
Fixed-price menus and à la carte: 80-150F.
Situated at the top of the Montagne Sainte-Geneviève, not far from the Panthéon, this restaurant will transport you to the springs and volcanos of the Auvergne. Meals are served in a light and airy room or in the peaceful inner garden, where you can enjoy a special regional dishes from the land of church bells, mountains and waterfalls. Be sure to have a look at the selection of Auvergne mineral waters.

La Fourmi ailée
8, Rue du Fouarre
☎ 01 43 29 40 99
Metro Saint-Michel
Open daily noon-midnight.
À la carte: 150F, including wine.
You'll get a friendly welcome at this restaurant situated near Notre-Dame. If you're looking for a peaceful evening try the mezzanine where the walls are lined with books. The cuisine itself is simple, but portions are very generous.

La Brouette et la Chandelle
41, Rue Descartes
☎ 01 43 25 41 10
Metro Cardinal Lemoine
Open daily 6-11.30pm.
Fixed price menus: 76-136F.
Enjoy a friendly evening with a raclette meal, melted cheese on potato or meat with salad, as much as you can eat for around 99F.

6th arrondissement

Le Six Huit
☎ 01 43 80 74 54
☎ 01 40 51 72 09
– Moored alongside the Quai Malaquais, opposite the Louvre
Open daily April to late Sept. for lunch and dinner
Metro St-Germain des Prés
– Moored alongside the Quai Montebello
Open Oct. to late March for dinner (closed Sun. and Mon.)
Metro St-Michel
À la carte: 200F, including wine.
Dine on a river barge, which is moored on the Seine opposite Notre-Dame for six months of the year, then near the Louvre during the winter. The upper deck is heated, but you can also sit in the Art Deco-style lower deck. Order the gambas flambéed in port, or clams sautéed in garlic, coriander and lemon. The Six Huit has concerts in the evenings (jazz, blues, pop and salsa) which you can enjoy with the Mediterranean cuisine.

7th arrondissement

Clémentine
62, Av. Bosquet
☎ 01 45 51 41 16
Metro École Militaire
Open daily (except Sat. lunch and Sun. dinner)
À la carte: 90F.
This traditional and trendy bistrot is decorated with advertising posters and photographs by Robert Doisneau.

La Fontaine de Mars
129, Rue St-Dominique
☎ 01 47 05 46 44
Metro École Militaire or Tour Maubourg
Open daily for lunch and dinner.
À la carte: 70-120F.
Just seconds away from the Eiffel Tower and the Champ de Mars, this restaurant serves specialities from the South-west, duck confit and honey-roasted duck magret (breast). The comfortable dining room upstairs overlooks the Mars Fountain.

8th arrondissement

Le Bec Rouge
33, Rue de Constantinople
☎ 01 45 22 15 02
Metro Villiers
Fixed-price menus and à la carte: 120-160F, including wine.
Try an authentic choucroute (sauerkraut) from Alsace and the ambiance of a Bierstube (beer bar). Situated in a residential quarter lined with imposing buildings, it's a great place to pop into if you're exploring the Parc Monceau or spending the afternoon shopping in the department stores along Boulevard Haussmann.

9th arrondissement

La Poste
22, Rue de Douai
☎ 01 45 26 50 00
Metro Blanche
Open every evening from 8pm.
À la carte: 200F.
This kitsch restaurant, just minutes from Place Pigalle, is the perfect place for a candlelit dinner. The red velvet, the gilded cherubs and the woodwork create a cosy ambiance, perfect for a chilly evening.

La Papaye bleue
89, Rue Lafayette
☎ 01 53 20 06 90
Metro Poissonière
Open daily 11am-10pm.
Fixed-price menu 69F, including cocktail and dessert.
Unusual and colourful painted wooden tables with collages made of shells, clay, beads and sand under glass. The menu matches the exotic decor.

Try Saum-tom salad (smoked salmon on warm blinis with avocado and palm hearts) served with a cocktail or a milkshake. The barman selects the fruit—pineapple, kiwi or passion fruit—and concocts a delicious drink just for you.

10th arrondissement

Chez Papa
206, Rue Lafayette
☎ 01 42 09 53 87
Metro Louis Blanc
Open daily for lunch and dinner
Fixed-price menu 50F, à la carte: under 100F.
In a friendly and relaxed ambiance, Chez Papa serves specialities from the South-west, cassoulet, a wide selection of snail dishes, and large salads based on duck, all excellent value.

11th arrondissement

L'Estaminet
116, Rue Oberkampf
☎ 01 43 57 34 29
Metro Ménilmontant or Parmentier
Open daily 7.30am-2am.
À la carte: 55-78F.
It would take more than one meal to try all the specialities from the Aveyron region in this bar/restaurant. To start, try the Pelou, an aperitif made with chestnut kirsch. Follow this with salmon or steak tartare, an Aveyronnais escalope, or the Estaminet salad, loaded with tomatoes, chicken liver, hot goat's cheese and sautéed potatoes. The restaurant has become a victim of its own success, and you may have to wait for a table.

Le Villaret
13, Rue Ternaux
☎ 01 43 57 89 76
Metro Parmentier
Open Mon.-Sat. for dinner
À la carte: 170F.
The menu changes every day here, depending on the market. The decor, with exposed beams and stone walls, is very atmospheric.

13th arrondissement

L'Olivier
18, Rue des Wallons
☎ 01 43 31 36 04
Metro St-Marcel
Open Mon.-Sat.
Fixed-price menus 90F, 115F for live music evenings.
Every evening, from Wednesday to Saturday, young pianists and violinists serenade diners with classical music. For those of you with a sweet tooth, note that the restaurant's manager won the Paris Grand Prix for his desserts.

Café Gladines
30, Rue des Cinq-Diamants
☎ 01 45 80 70 10
Metro Corvisart
Open daily 9am-2am
Fixed-price lunch menu: 60F, à la carte: 35-80F.
A great place to come for salads with magret or confit de canard (duck) and other specialities from the South-west, served in a Basque decor.

La Virgule
9, Rue Véronèse
☎ 01 43 37 01 14
Metro Place d'Italie
Open daily for lunch and dinner (except Sun. lunch).
Fixed-price menu and à la carte: 60-200F.
An Asian run restaurant serving French food in copious portions and with great imagination.

La Guinguette Pirate
Quai de la Gare
☎ 01 44 24 89 89
Metro Quai de la Gare
Open Tue.-Sun. 8.30pm-midnight.
À la carte: 65-80F.
The barge, moored near the Bibliothèque de France opposite Bercy, still looks like an old outdoor dance hall. Choose a table on the upper wooden deck or inside, and enjoy a plate of cheese, a selection of cakes or a full meal. Concerts (usually reggae or rock) are held in the evenings from 9.30pm. Storytellers and puppet shows entertain the children on Wednesday and Saturday afternoons at 3.30 pm.

RESTAURANTS

15th arrondissement

Bermuda Onion
16, Rue Linois
01 45 75 11 11
Metro Charles-Michels
Open daily for dinner,
Sun. for lunch
À la carte: 100-150F.
The view overlooking the Seine is fantastic, the decor is unique and the menu, interesting and varied. The entrance, was inspired by the film Basic Instinct.

Le Brasier
58, Rue Olivier de Serres
☎ 01 45 31 25 66
Metro Convention or
Porte de Versailles
Open daily for lunch
and dinner.
50-100F.
Here you sit around a grill and cook your own brochette (kebab), meat and cheese.

16th arrondissement

Flo Prestiges
61, Av. de la Grande
Armée
☎ 01 45 00 12 10
Open daily 9.30am-11pm.
À la carte: 50-100F.
If you feel like staying in and still want a delicious dinner, just call and order any number of special dishes which are delivered right to your door. Portions are available for one to six people. Order the daily or weekend special. The menu changes every two weeks. You can also order wine and dessert. A meal, including delivery within Paris, will cost from 100 to 130F. You can also buy directly from the shop.

17th arrondissement

Chez Tof
117, Rue des Dames
☎ 01 43 87 63 08
Open Mon-Sat (excluding lunch Sat.)
Fixed-price menus:
65-89F.
This is an establishment run by an unusual and jovial chef, proud of his specialities from the South-west which include foie gras, confits, grilled meat and homemade cassoulets on Friday and Saturday. The

enormous salads, served in individual salad bowls, are daunting. Tradition has it that anyone who doesn't clean his plate buys the owner a drink (although he tends to be lenient with female guests). Big eaters are served a second portion. The price is great value given the quality, quantity and overall good humour.

18th arrondissement

Sortie de Secours
32 bis, Rue des Trois
Frères
☎ 01 42 57 27 66
Metro Abbesses
Open Tue.-Sun.
30F per dish.
This small tapas restaurant will always welcome you with a smile.

Le Kokolion
62, Rue d'Orsel
☎ 01 42 58 24 41
Metro Abbesses
Open every evening
until 1am.
Fixed-price menus: 89-139F, à la carte: 80F.
This restaurant is situated near the Théâtre de l'Atelier. You can order the goats' cheeses, honey-roasted duck or tasty chocolate dessert until 1 am.

La Pomponnette
42, Rue Lepic
☎ 01 46 06 08 36
Metro Abbesses, Blanche
Open daily for lunch
and dinner (except
Mon. lunch and Sun.)
Fixed-price menus:
100-175F, including wine.
À la carte: 200-220F.
This decor of this turn of the century restaurant has been kept intact by the descendants of the original owner. The walls are lined with paintings by artists, left as payment for their meals. The cuisine is typically French (calf's head, haricot mutton (a type of Irish stew), and is appreciated as much by locals as by tourists.

19th arrondissement

Le Brasier
101, Av. Jean-Jaurès
☎ 01 42 00 10 98
Metro Laumière

Open daily for lunch and
dinner.
50-100F.
A DIY dinner where a grill is placed in the centre of the table and you cook own meat, or have a raclette, a dish where you melt cheese onto potato or meat, very filling.

20th arrondissement

La Mère Lachaise
78 Bd Ménilmontant
☎ 01 47 97 61 60
Metro Père-Lachaise or
Ménilmontant
Open daily 9am-2am.
This is a pleasant unpretentious place with old furniture and lamps. Lunch and dinner portions are generous and very good value. The 85F Sunday brunch menu is excellent. You can enjoy eating on the terrace in the summer.

RESTAURANTS

1st arrondissement

La Cloche des Halles
28, Rue Coquillière
Metro Les Halles
☎ 01 42 36 93 89
Open Mon.-Fri. 8am-
10pm; Sat. 10am-5pm.
Closed Sat. evening and
Sun.
50F per main dish.
*Everything here is homemade.
The owners of this wine bar buy
their wines directly from the
vineyards and bring it back in
oak casks and bottle it themselves. To accompany these
excellent wines, enjoy generous
servings of charcuterie and
cheese. Finish off with homemade tarts and cakes.*

2nd arrondissement

La Grappe d'Orgueil
5, Rue des Petits
Carreaux
Metro Sentier, Les Halles
☎ 01 40 13 00 17
Open Tues.-Sun for lunch
and dinner.
Main dish: 50F.
*This old bistrot, lined with
mirrors, was opened in the
1930s. Musicians entertain
the guests once a week.*

3rd arrondissement

L'Apparement Café
18, Rue Coutures St-
Gervais
Metro St-Sébastien-
Froissart
☎ 01 48 87 12 22
Open Mon.-Fri. noon-
2am, Sat. 4pm-2am,
Sun. noon-midnight.
Main dish: 48-75F.
*This café looks more like an
apartment. Settle in one of the
sofas or comfortable armchairs
and sip a cocktail or play a board
game. If you're looking for soli-
tude, plunge into the collection
of old Paris Match magazines at
the back of the room. Cosy and
friendly ambiance.*

4th arrondissement

**Au Bourguignon
du Marais**
19, Rue de Jouy
Metro Saint-Paul or
Pont-Marie
☎ 01 48 87 15 40

Open Mon.-Fri. noon-
11pm.
À la carte: 115F.
Wine: 160-300F per
bottle, 25-42F per glass.
*If you're a Bordeaux fan, this is
not the place for you. Everyone
in this wine bar sits on bamboo
chairs around simple wooden
tables drinking Burgundy wines.*

Au Petit Fer à Cheval
30, Rue Vieille du Temple
Metro Hôtel de Ville
☎ 01 42 72 47 47
Open daily 9am-2am.
Sandwiches: 20-30F.
*This old bistrot is in a building
that has been classified as a
historical monument and is
decorated with mirrors and
lights. It has one of the last
horseshoe-shaped zinc bars
left in Paris.*

Enoteca
25, Rue Charles-V
Metro Saint-Paul
☎ 01 42 78 91 44
Open daily noon-midnight.
Wine: 90-800F per bottle,
20-45F per glass.
*Enjoy one of the 300 Italian
wines on the list as you sit in the
high-ceilinged room with exposed beams and lovely woodwork. The service is friendly,
and a new selection of wine by
the glass is offered each week:
one aperitif, two white wines,
five red wines, a rosé and a
sweet wine. The Enoteca is also
a restaurant, with a weekly
menu that includes five pasta
dishes and three main dishes to
accompany your wine.*

5th arrondissement

Finnegans Wake
9, Rue des Boulangers
Metro Jussieu
☎ 01 46 34 23 65
Open Mon.-Fri. 11am-
2am, Sat.-Sun 6pm-2am.
Beer: 25-35F per pint.
*This pub serves all sorts of
beers—Adel, Blanche, Guiness,
Kinkenny—in a friendly ambiance.
Blues and country bands play
on Friday nights in the cellar.
The pub organises language
classes on evenings during the
week (Gaelic, Welsh) at 7.30pm,
and poetry readings on Sundays
at 7.30pm.*

6th arrondissement

Le Bar
27, Rue Condé
Metro Odéon,
Luxembourg
☎ 01 43 29 06 61
Open evenings to 3-4am.
*Sip a cocktail and play chess
or backgammon, under the
watchful eyes of the Buddhas
and Chinese statues.*

La Rhumerie
166, Bd Saint-Germain
Metro Mabillon
☎ 01 43 54 28 94
Open daily 9am-2am.
Cocktails: 30F.
*This establishment has been in
business since 1932, and the
tradition has been passed from
father to daughter. You'll find
all sorts of cocktails made with
rum, including daiquiris and
punches. If you're feeling
peckish, try the Creole dishes
washed down with a glass of
punch for 70F.*

8th arrondissement

Barfly
49-51 Av. Georges V
Metro Georges V
☎ 01 53 67 84 60
Daily noon-3pm, 7pm-
2am. Closed Sat. lunch.
*This bar, in the heart of the 8th
arrondissement, is the ideal
place to see and be seen.
The prices go hand in hand with
the very smart area near the
Georges V hotel, so beware.*

11th arrondissement

Scarbo
1, a, Passage Saint-
Sébastien
Metro Sébastien-Froissart
☎ 01 47 00 58 59
Open Mon.-Fri. 10am-
2am, weekends, 6pm-
2am.
Fixed-price lunch menu
50F.
*This classic old Parisian café is
in an interesting alley and has
recently been taken over by
young owners who have retained the original decor (often
used as a film set). The walls are
lined with photographs or paintings. The menu changes daily,
and evenings are reserved for
concerts or poetry readings.*

12th arrondissement

Le Viaduc Café
43, Av. Daumesnil
Metro Gare de Lyon
☎ 01 44 74 70 70
Open daily to 3am.
À la carte: 100-150F.
Follow the 'Coulée verte', a former viaduct that has been transformed into a suspended garden running from the Bastille to the Bois de Vincennes. The Viaduc des Arts is on Avenue Daumesnil. As you explore the many shops under the archways, take a break at this café and enjoy a Sunday brunch with jazz.

17th arrondissement

James Joyce
71, Bd Gouvion-St-Cyr
Metro Porte Maillot
☎ 01 44 09 70 32
Open daily 7am-midnight.
Beer: 20-50F.
With a name like James Joyce, you know this must be an Irish pub. The young Irish bartenders serve beer from their home country.

18th arrondissement

L'Alibi
11, Rue Lapeyrère
Metro Jules Joffrin
☎ 01 42 52 23 50
Open Tue.-Sat. 5.30pm-1.45am
Drinks: from 12F.
This brasserie is in a former turn of the century wood and coal storehouse and has retained the original setting, with huge glass windows. Choose from beer, wine or Cuban rum to accompany your salad, plate of charcuterie (cooked pork meats) or selection of cheeses.

Café aux Noctambules
24, Bd de Clichy
Metro Pigalle
☎ 01 46 06 16 38
Open daily 9am-4.30am (except Sun. evening).
Starting at 10pm every night, Pierre Carré entertains guests with his repertoire of French songs from 1900 onwards. He will also do requests, so don't feel shy to ask.

La Divette de Montmatre
136, Rue Marcadet
Metro Marcadet-Poissonniers
☎ 01 46 06 19 64
Open Mon.-Sat. noon-1am.
Beer: from 13F.
This bar is decorated entirely in old vinyl records and is extremely popular with the locals.

Le Sancerre
35, Rue des Abbesses
Metro Abbesses
☎ 01 42 58 08 20
Open daily 7:30am-2am.
Plates of cheese and charcuterie (cooked pork meats): 50F.
This is an original Parisian bistrot, with old photographs and musical instruments hanging on the walls. Choose from a large selection of wine and beer on tap. The house favourite is the Cuban cocktail known as 'Morito'.

BARS

NOTES

HACHETTE TRAVEL GUIDES

Titles available in this series:

A GREAT WEEKEND IN PARIS (ISBN: 1 84202 001 3)
A GREAT WEEKEND IN AMSTERDAM (ISBN: 1 84202 002 1)
A GREAT WEEKEND IN ROME (ISBN: 1 84202 003 X)
A GREAT WEEKEND IN NEW YORK (ISBN: 1 84202 004 8)
A GREAT WEEKEND IN BARCELONA (ISBN: 1 84202 005 6)
A GREAT WEEKEND IN PRAGUE (ISBN: 1 84202 000 5)

Also to be published in 2000
A GREAT WEEKEND IN FLORENCE (ISBN: 1 84202 010 2)
A GREAT WEEKEND IN LISBON (ISBN: 1 84202 011 0)
A GREAT WEEKEND IN NAPLES (ISBN: 1 84202 016 1)
A GREAT WEEKEND IN LONDON (ISBN: 1 84202 013 7)
A GREAT WEEKEND IN BERLIN (ISBN: 1 84202 061 7)
A GREAT WEEKEND IN BRUSSELS (ISBN: 1 84202 017 X)
A GREAT WEEKEND IN VENICE (ISBN: 1 84202 018 8)
A GREAT WEEKEND IN VIENNA (ISBN: 1 84202 026 9)

HACHETTE VACANCES
Who better to write about France than the French?
A series of colourful, information-packed, leisure and activity guides
for family holidays by French authors. Literally hundreds of suggestions
for things to do and sights to see per title.

To be published in 2000
PROVENCE & THE COTE D'AZUR (ISBN: 1 84202 006 4)
BRITTANY (ISBN: 1 84202 007 2)
LANGUEDOC-ROUSSILLON (ISBN: 1 84202 008 0)
POITOU-CHARENTES (ISBN: 1 84202 009 9)
SOUTH-WEST FRANCE (ISBN: 1 84202 014 5)
PYRENEES & GASCONY (ISBN: 1 84202 015 3)

ROUTARD
Comprehensive and reliable guides offering insider advice for the
independent traveller.

To be published from Summer 2000
PARIS (ISBN: 1 84202 027 7)
PROVENCE & THE COTE D'AZUR (ISBN: 1 84202 019 6)
BRITTANY (ISBN: 1 84202 020 X)
ANDALUCIA (ISBN: 1 84202 028 5)
SOUTHERN ITALY, ROME & SICILY (ISBN: 1 84202 021 8)
GREEK ISLANDS & ATHENS (ISBN: 1 84202 023 4)
IRELAND (ISBN: 1 84202 024 2)
CALIFORNIA, NEVADA & ARIZONA (ISBN: 1 84202 025 0)
BELGIUM (ISBN: 1 84202 022 6)
THAILAND (ISBN: 1 84202 029 3)
CUBA (ISBN: 1 84202 062 5)
WEST CANADA & ONTARIO (ISBN: 1 84202 031 5)